STAND & WITHSTAND INTEGRITY GROUP
AN EDUCATIONAL VALUE CONTINUUM™ RESOURCE

THE SUPPLY

EDUCATION REFORM WE NEED
PERPETUATED BY EDUCATORS WHO LEAD

SUPPLY IT
WHAT "TEACHING IS A NOBLE PROFESSION" REALLY MEANS
DANIEL C. MANLEY

SUPPLY IT
WHAT "TEACHING IS A NOBLE PROFESSION" REALLY MEANS
WORKBOOK
DANIEL C. MANLEY

DESIGN IT
WHAT "TODAY'S LESSON WILL BE ABOUT..." REALLY MEANS
EDUCATIONAL PLANNING GUIDE
DANIEL C. MANLEY

Library of Congress Cataloging-in-Publication Data has been applied for.
ISBN 978-1-7369736-9-1 (Paperback)

Printed in the United States of America

First Edition January 2022

P.O. Box 782771
Wichita, KS 67278
STANDWITHSTAND.ORG

CONTENTS

HOW DO I USE THIS PLANNING GUIDE ii

    Am I Leading, Provoking, And Supporting An Educational Pursuit? ii

    Did I Facilitate The Educational Process And Fulfill The Mission Of Educating? v

    Progress Report v

    Educational Value Continuum™ Minimum Functionality vi

    Educational Value Continuum™ Maximum Possibility vii

    Supply & Demand Education™ viii

    Attendance & Instruction ix

    Attendance Level Assessment x

    Instructional Level Assessment xi

    Educational Pursuit Evaluation xii

    Educational Provision Evaluation xiv

    Education Receipt xvi

SEMESTER #1 ....

    Unit Timeline ....

    Weekly Plans ....

    Semester Progress Report ....

SEMESTER #2 ....

    Unit Timeline ....

    Weekly Plans ....

    Semester Progress Report ....

GLOSSARY OF TERMS ....

ABOUT THE AUTHOR ....

DEDICATION ....

HOW DO I USE THIS PLANNING GUIDE?

As an educator, it is of the utmost importance that you possess, understand, know how to use, and benefit from materials and tools designed to assist you in leading, provoking, and supporting students in pursuit of an education. This planning guide is to serve as an additional resource to *Supply It: What "Teaching Is A Noble Profession" Really Means.* While reading that book, the strict emphasis that needs to be placed on all four components of an education, in order for one to be considered an educator who facilitates an experience that qualifies as educational, should have been made clear to you. You were informed that:

> "Your ability to answer these two never-ending questions is a clear indication of how well you have planned and executed an educational experience for your students. 'Am I leading, provoking, and supporting an educational pursuit,' and 'Did I facilitate the educational process and fulfill the mission of education,' are altruistic questions that require you to ensure your students an educational experience. Remember, they cannot consider themselves educated unless they can confirm having all four components of an education. Thus, you cannot consider yourself to be an educator unless you can confirm presenting all four components of an education to them."

You owe it to yourself, as the teaching profession has yet to make education the standard, to be able to gauge the effectiveness of your practice with an accountability measure created, solely, for the purpose of mandating that educational value be built-in to every lesson. Being able to confirm this makes it nearly impossible for you to miss the educational target and deprive students of an educational experience. With *that* level of importance, strategic planning must go into developing an experience that is educationally grounded. You must ***Design It***. In doing so, you provide yourself with documentation of the experience and a catalogued inventory of the educational value that it offered. Ending a semester, school year, or K-12 academic career and realizing that *education* was missed in the experience is a vulnerable position that triggers blame inquisitions. Validating a demand for you, the educator, to do more, better, or different will be nearly impossible for anyone if you can answer these questions affirmatively.

Am I Leading, Provoking, And Supporting An Educational Pursuit?

What educators are really trying to figure out by asking themselves this question is, "How do I design a lesson that provides a true educational experience and upholds the nobility of the profession." A lesson that, to a caregiver or teacher, might seem to be engaging, enjoyable, and educational, could still be void of any number of educational components. This one question, "Am I leading, provoking, and supporting an educational pursuit," is really a way to standardize and maintain the educational integrity of any instruction that students are subjected to. If a lesson is going to be a part of a student's *educational* experience, within the *education* system, the *educational value* of that lesson must be apparent to all participants of the educational process. Planning to facilitate such an experience must, indeed, be calculated.

HOW DO I USE THIS PLANNING GUIDE?

Weekly Planning

The layout of this planning guide provides you with four individual lesson templates for every week of the school year. How you go about differentiating and utilizing those spaces is to be determined by your unique scheduling and instructional needs (by day, class period, attendee/academic levels, special education accommodations, educational components, etc.). This planning guide, specifically, is meant to be used for one content area. Thus, if you teach 3 different subjects/preps/courses, you will likely need 3 different planning guides to supplement each separately. The respective sections of each template can be broken down accordingly:

1) Standard – what academic benchmark or content objective is the focus of instruction?

2) Content – what specific subject matter is being used to guide/root instruction academically?

3) Designation – for what audience, purpose, day, or in what way is this lesson differentiated?

4) Unit – what is the overall section of your content/discipline that this week's lessons are a part of?

5) Week Of – what calendar days are the lessons included on these two pages meant to cover?

EXPOSE

In accordance with the Educational Value Continuum™, what is the educational value of the lesson you have planned?

1) EVC Minimum – what Minimum Functionality element(s) should learners look forward to adding to, or enhancing within, their educational repertoire because of this instruction/learning?

2) EVC Maximum – what Maximum Possibility element(s) should learners look forward to adding to, or enhancing within, their educational repertoire because of this instruction/learning?

EXPLORE

In what ways and with what tools are you planning on facilitating learning and allowing students to pursue their education?

1) Activities – what planned method(s) of instruction will you be utilizing to teach material?

2) Strategies – how, specifically, will you structure and/or execute those activities to maximize their impact on planned activities and the educational experience in the room?

3) Materials – what tools, equipment, or other resources are necessary to accomplish these tasks?

EXPERIENCE

What is the expected result of the instruction/experience students are being made to go along with?

1) Knowledge & Competence – what should students, on the most fundamental level, be able to say, do, and prove once instruction and learning have taken place?

2) Assignments / Assessments / EVC Statements – what will be used to measure the level at which students are learning (allowing them to demonstrate how well their educational pursuit and acquisition are going)?

HOW DO I USE THIS PLANNING GUIDE?

<u>ENGAGE</u>

In what ways will students be expected to work, actively, as they pursue an education, and what hurdles do you anticipate preventing them from being able to do so with relative ease?

1) Necessary Activity – what is the most common way students will be required to invest energy and effort into their pursuit?

> THINK – making the mind (intellectual processing) the most active tool in an educational pursuit.
>
> DO – making hands (writing), mouth (talking), or other body part (movement/activity) the most active tool in an educational pursuit.
>
> SEE – making the eyes (watching/viewership) the most active tool in an educational pursuit.
>
> LISTEN – making the ears (hearing) the most active tool in an educational pursuit.

2) Likely Questions – what do you foresee students being curious about or confused by – how do you plan on responding to this line of questioning?

3) Likely Difficulty – what do you foresee students struggling with or being put off by – how do you plan on scaffolding for and alleviating these obstacles?

<u>EXCITES</u>

For what reason(s) should students embrace this opportunity and see this particular instruction/learning as something worth investing in personally?

1) Cultural – what about your student's personal, historical, ethnic, and social experience should connect them to this instruction/learning?

2) Developmental – what about your student's psychological and physiological evolution should connect them to this instruction/learning?

3) Individual – what interests, hobbies, or desires do your students have, mutually or independently, that you can emphasize to better connect them with this instruction/learning?

Instructional Level Assessment and Educational Provision Evaluation:

An educator who does not take time to judge and take inventory of that which they are offering students at school is most likely to be unsuccessful in their role. To be unsuccessful as an educator is to be unable to say, "I provided my students with a safe, appropriate space and opportunity to acquire a unique assortment of information that they could possess, understand, know how to use, and benefit from – I guarantee it," at the end of a student's tenure. By reflecting on, rating, and recording your performance levels on a weekly basis, performing beneath the level of an educator, and offering less than a complete education, becomes increasingly difficult to do. Use the *Instructional Level Assessment* and *Educational Provision Evaluation* tools at the end of each week of instruction to hold yourself accountable for facilitating the educational process and fulfilling the mission of education. You have also been provided the mirroring *Attendance Level Assessment* and *Educational Pursuit Evaluation* tools to assess the efficiency levels your students are performing at. Greater than a "grade" received, the absolute value of the education acquired will be validated and legitimized with these tools.

HOW DO I USE THIS PLANNING GUIDE?

Did I Facilitate The Educational Process And Fulfill The Mission of Education?

What educators are really trying to figure out by asking themselves this question is, "How successful was I in my effort to lead, provoke, and support an educational pursuit." When academic content is presented by caregivers and teachers, rarely do they include the final two components of an education. Consequently, being void of half of that which constitutes an education, even lessons that have gone according to plan cannot be deemed successful. In order to measure success on an educational pursuit (student) or educational provision effort (educator), utilize the included evaluation tools and rubrics to gauge the overall effectiveness with clarity and precision. By grading yourself (on a weekly basis), and allowing students the same opportunity, the absolute value of the facilitated educational experience should be made clear to all participants. This one question, "Did I facilitate the educational process and fulfill the mission of education," is really a way to standardize and maintain accountability throughout the entirety of the educational experience.

Progress Report:

Over the course of a semester, much activity, learning, growth, and educating *should* be occurring. A full schoolyear offers too much to grasp an understanding of at the year's end. Failing to keep record of the daily happenings of your school days will allow for semesters, school years, and academic levels to pass with no evidence of learning. By reflecting on your record every semester and taking note of patterns and trends as they occur, you will be able to adjust as needed and maximize your ability to effectively facilitate an educational experience. Complete these six statements with information based on your careful consideration of the semesters plans and how well you believe those plans led to a high-quality educational experience for your students:

1) When I reflect on what I EXPOSED students to this semester, I see that…

2) When I reflect on what and how I let students EXPLORE this semester, I see that…

3) When I reflect on the EXPERIENCE I provided students with this semester, I see that…

4) When I reflect on how I required/allowed students to ENGAGE this semester, I see that…

5) When I reflect on what I did to EXCITE students this semester, I see that…

6) When I reflect on my EDUCATIONAL PROVISION and INSTRUCTIONAL LEVEL, I see that…

While reflecting, consider each of these four aspects for each of the ten statements as they apply:

1) I was successful… – what went well consistently, where did you shine, keep the good things going?

2) I really struggled… – what is not working, where are you stressed, where are improvements needed?

3) Moving forward… – what adjustments should be made to classes, instructors, relationships, habits, etc.?

4) I may need my allies… – feeling incapable, unheard, unsafe, or unproductive in any area; what help do you need?

EDUCATIONAL VALUE CONTINUUM™

Minimum Functionality:

On the most basic level, what purpose does the study of this subject and support material serve in my life (now or in the foreseeable future) that benefits me directly?

1) **Ability** – offers the power or capability to do.
   Learners Say: "I now know how to ____ and can ____."
   Example: "I now know how to <u>compose a thesis statement</u> and can <u>articulate a strong argument or stance for any opinion I have</u>."

2) **Skill** – raises the level and proficiency of an ability already possessed.
   Learners Say: "I am now better at ____."
   Example: "I am now better at <u>supporting my personal opinion with evidence from credible sources</u>."

3) **Vocation** – develops the understanding of a certain job, profession, or business.
   Learners Say: "I now know (what / what a) ____ (are / is) and (do / does)."
   Example: "I now know what an <u>anesthesiologist</u> is and does."

4) **Relationship** – develops the understanding of human connection, interaction, and involvement.
   Learners Say: "I can now (relate better to / better understand the / more easily) ____ because of ____."
   Example: "I can now relate better to <u>people who are different</u> because of <u>a lesson on World War II and the Holocaust</u>."

5) **Mentality** – challenges, changes, composes, or confirms personal perspectives on life or the world.
   Learners Say: "My ideas about ____ (are now / have been) ____ due to ____."
   Example: "My ideas about <u>gun control</u> are now <u>more progressive</u> due to <u>mass shooting statistics</u>."

6) **Mental Exercise** – works, conditions, or trains the brain for better overall functionality.
   Learners Say: "I am able (to / to do) ____ (better / more) because I have exercised my mind."
   Example: "I am able to <u>make rational decisions</u> more quickly because I have exercised my mind."

7) **Muscle Memory** – works, conditions, or trains the physical body for better overall functionality.
   Learners Say: "I am able (to / to do) ____ (better / more) ____ because I have exercised my body."
   Example: "I am able to <u>be active without pain or fatigue</u> more because I have exercised my body."

8) **Practice** – provides time and opportunity to raise competence or effectiveness of an ability.
   Learners Say: "I worked to improve my ____ by ____."
   Example: "I worked to improve my <u>diction and ability to project</u> by <u>doing vocal warmups in choir</u>."

9) **Training** – provides purposeful, more disciplined, focused, and intensive practice of a specific ability to become more skilled.
   Learners Say: "I worked to improve my ____ by ____."
   Example: "I worked to improve my <u>attention to detail</u> by <u>measuring ingredients for a recipe</u>."

10) **Experience** – encountering and becoming more familiar in order to raise one's awareness or aptitude.
    Learners Say: "I spent time ____ to be (better / more) ____ (at / with / of) ____."
    Example: "I spent time <u>working with a group</u> to be more <u>knowledgeable</u> of <u>how well people with different personalities can work together</u>."

EDUCATIONAL VALUE CONTINUUM™

Maximum Possibility:

At the most accomplished and advanced level, what purpose could the study of this subject and support material serve in my life and what beneficial position could it ultimately land me in?

1) **Motivation** – creates or causes a reason to act.
   Learners Say: "I now have a (desire / stronger desire) to ____."
   Example: "I now have a stronger desire to <u>manage my finances well enough to retire young</u>."

2) **Inspiration** – sparks or ignites an internal motivation.
   Learners Say: "I feel ____ compelling me to ____."
   Example: "I feel <u>the restrictions on past generations</u> compelling me to <u>surpass what limited them</u>."

3) **Higher Education** – instills the desire to pursue an education past the high school level.
   Learners Say: "I want to go to ____ and study ____ (to / so that) ____."
   Example: "I want to go to <u>art school</u> and study <u>graphic design</u> so that <u>I can start my own branding company</u>."

4) **Career** – instills the desire to pursue a specific profession or occupation.
   Learners Say: "I want to (be a / work for) ____ so that I can ____."
   Example: "I want to be a <u>zoologist</u> so that I can work with <u>endangered populations</u>."

5) **Dream** – instills the desire to pursue a grandiose goal, passion, or vision.
   Learners Say: "I want (to / to be) ____ and one day ____."
   Example: "I want to be <u>a marine</u> and one day <u>become Sergeant Major of the Marine Corps</u>."

6) **Invention** – stimulates the imagination to create something that did not exist previously.
   Learners Say: "I want to create (a / the) ____ that (can / will) ____."
   Example: "I want to create a <u>waste disposal method</u> that will <u>be good for the environment</u>."

7) **Innovation** – stimulates the imagination to create something newer than the already established.
   Learners Say: "I want to improve ____ so that (it / it can) ____."
   Example: "I want to improve <u>solar technology</u> so that it can <u>help fight against climate change</u>."

8) **Non-Profit** – motivates one to establish, develop, and pursue goals meant to provide a public service or benefit.
   Learners Say: "I want to help ____ so they will be able to ____."
   Example: "I want to help <u>the homeless</u> so they will be able to <u>live stable and productive lives</u>."

9) **Fortune-500** – motivates one to establish, develop, and pursue goals meant to gain significant financial wealth.
   Learners Say: "I want to become ____ and acquire ____."
   Example: "I want to become <u>CEO of a major corporation</u> and acquire <u>7-figure gains annually</u>."

10) **Superhero** – motivates one to establish, develop, and pursue goals meant to effect positive change on the largest possible scale.
    Learners Say: "I want to impact and improve ____ by ____."
    Example: "I want to impact and improve <u>the probability of people living fulfilled lives</u> by <u>helping them to secure for themselves a high-quality education at the earliest possible age</u>."

SUPPLY & DEMAND EDUCATION™

PHILOSOPHY:

If we can quantify education, then we can measure it. If we can measure education, then we can guarantee it. If we can guarantee education, it should come with a warranty. Cultivating a space where educational demand and educational supply are equal in quantity, obstacles to the acquiring of an education should be easy to recognize and, thus, remove. Supply & Demand Education™ eliminates the scarcity of a high-quality educational experience as equilibrium is clear and profitable to both producer and consumer.

QUESTION:

"Why do I have to take this class," is an evidential question exposing a learner's desire to know the educational value of presented material. Do not allow yourself to take the cynical viewpoint that the individual asking this question is a troublemaker, lazy, unappreciative, or stupid. "Why do I have to study...," whatever course, content, or subject that is in question, is the inarticulate plea of an individual who is saying desperately, "Help me understand how I can use and benefit from this content so I can appreciate and take advantage of the opportunity I have been given to learn it."

ANSWER:

To expose you to, let you explore, and provide experience with the functions and possibilities of...," whatever course, content, or subject that is in question, is the articulate response of an educator who is qualified to lead students through the complete educational process. Doing so guarantees provision of a quality educational experience.

PROCESS:

1) **EXPOSE Them To It** – Awareness:

   Initiating an encounter between the functions and possibilities of an academic discipline, practical ability, or vocational skill set and the ignorance, inexperience, and curiosity of a student.

2) **Let Them EXPLORE It** – Analysis:

   Developing a cultivated space and opportunity for students to investigate, manipulate, and question the functions and possibilities of an academic discipline, practical ability, or vocational skill set.

3) **Once They EXPERIENCE It** – Application:

   Facilitating student attainment of a basic knowledge and competency of the functions and possibilities of an academic discipline, practical ability, or vocational skill set.

4) **They Will ENGAGE In** – Agency:

   Working actively to add the functions and possibilities of an academic discipline, practical ability, or vocational skill set to one's own educational repertoire.

5) **That Which EXCITES Them** – Ambition:

   Possessing and exhibiting unique interest in the functions and possibilities of an academic discipline, practical ability, or vocational skill set.

ATTENDANCE & INSTRUCTION

We must acknowledge that not every individual in attendance at an academic institution is looking to fulfill the primary purpose for which they were admitted. It must also be accepted that not every person facilitating instruction within those buildings is fulfilling the primary purpose for which their position was meant. The options below are not meant to judge character, but identify the focus of individual intentions. While reciprocal needs and allowances are most likely to be met while attendees and instructors are on identical levels, the ability to adapt *to* and make accommodations *for* all levels will offer each participant the best opportunity for success. Also, positioning on any particular level is more fluid than static. Thus, movement up, as well as down, is expected to occur for various reasons.

Attendance Levels:

Schools are meant to be institutions that provide students with space and opportunity to pursue and acquire an education. The peak performance of any school can only be reached when occupants operate, at the very least, as "students." However, five varieties of young people will enter an academic institution each day:

1) **Child** – has no direct interest in learning or education; having their basic needs met is their most pressing concern.

2) **Pupil** – is willing to take part in learning but has no defined goals or ambition educationally; they will comply, they will participate, but intrinsic motivation is lacking substantially.

3) **Student** – actively engages in the pursuit of an education and desires, ultimately, to be educated.

4) **Active Participant** – an advanced persona assumed by the student, making them energetic and optimistic in pursuit of a high-quality education; they aspire to have, above all else, an education to secure success in life.

5) **Engaged Agent** – the highest persona to be assumed by a student, making them eager and expectant while working to acquire the fullness of educational possibility; perfected competence is what they pursue.

Instructional Levels:

Teaching is meant to be a noble profession where educators maximize the space and opportunity afforded to students by leading, provoking, and supporting their educational pursuits. The peak performance of any school can only be reached when instructors operate, at the very least, as "educators." However, five varieties of instructor are tasked with facilitating the experience of those who attend academic institutions:

1) **Caregiver** – does not focus on nor do they emphasize education; the provision of childcare is what they prioritize most as they look to meet the basic needs of a child.

2) **Teacher** – actively promotes instruction and enables learning, but they do not identify or achieve specific educational goals; they know their job - they do their job - they focus on the job.

3) **Educator** – leads, provokes, and supports students in the pursuit of an education and desires, ultimately, for them to be educated.

4) **Profound Mentor** – an advanced persona assumed by the educator, making them insightful and practical as they infuse a high-quality educational experience with lessons designed to prepare students for success in life.

5) **Intense Trainer** – the highest persona to be assumed by an educator, making them astute and extremely proficient while working to bring to fruition the richest and most rewarding educational experience possible.

ATTENDANCE LEVEL ASSESSMENT

While school is meant to be an institution that provides students with space and opportunity to pursue and acquire an education, there are five varieties of young people who enter the building each day. Answer the five questions below and add each of the numbers represented by your selected answer to find out which categorical level you are currently attending school at. Do know that your overall attendance level may be different when dealing with a particular subject, instructor, activity, or situation. However, the score you receive here represents your most general attendance level. Note: your most honest answers are those that reflect your fundamental beliefs and dictate actions, not your idealistic aspirations.

My Attitude About School Attendance Is This:
1) I would much rather be somewhere else.
2) Having to go to school does not irritate me much.
3) Attending school, for educational reasons, is something that I enjoy.
4) I greatly appreciate having space and opportunity to pursue an education.
5) Having space and opportunity to acquire an education makes school my favorite place to be.

My Attitude About Schoolwork And Assignments Is This:
1) Most of the assignments and academic tasks that I am given annoy me.
2) Whenever I am given work to do, I usually just do it.
3) I try hard to get something out of the work I am assigned to do.
4) Giving me a chance to become more educated excites me and sparks my interest.
5) Any opportunity to strengthen my education is appreciated and taken advantage of fully.

My Attitude About Assessment Scores And Grades Is This:
1) The scores and grades I receive really do not affect me.
2) I like to get good ones, but the bad ones have little influence on me.
3) They are a good way to see what I have truly learned.
4) When content is understood at the level I desire, my grades will reflect the education I have.
5) I am likely to ask questions about any completed task that earns less than 100%.

My Attitude About Classroom Instructors And Administration Is This:
1) The way they always try to tell me what to do gets on my nerves.
2) If they don't bother me, then I don't bother them.
3) The work that they do makes my education possible.
4) They deserve the utmost respect for the work they do and opportunities they provide.
5) What they provide allows me to build a foundation for my future; I am very much in need of their diligence.

My Attitude About Social Interactions And Extracurricular Activities Is This:
1) School is not worth attending without them.
2) Most of what I enjoy about school is connected to these.
3) They add to my education in a different way, but they are still beneficial.
4) For what my educational pursuit requires of me, these are much needed supports.
5) If they complement my educational pursuit, I will invest in them. If not, I can and will do without them.

5-9	10-14	15-19	20-24	25
Child	Pupil	Student	Active Participant	Engaged Agent

INSTRUCTIONAL LEVEL ASSESSMENT

While teaching is meant to be a noble profession where educators maximize the space and opportunity afforded to students by leading, provoking, and supporting an educational pursuit, five varieties of instructor are tasked with facilitating the experience of those who attend school each day. Answer the five questions below and add each of the numbers represented by your selected answer to find out which categorical level you are instructing at. Do know that your overall instructional level may be different when dealing with a particular subject, young person, activity, or situation. However, the score you receive here represents your most general instructional level. Note: your most honest answers are those that reflect your fundamental beliefs and dictate actions, not your idealistic aspirations.

My Attitude About Teaching Is This:
1) Seeing young people grow and have fun at school brings me joy.
2) It is very rewarding when teaching and learning take place and the job gets done.
3) Leading, provoking, and supporting students on their educational pursuit is the mission.
4) Maximizing the space and opportunity meant for students to acquire an education is my purpose.
5) I am responsible for providing a complete understanding of how useful and beneficial my content can be.

My Attitude About Schoolwork And Assignments Is This:
1) A variety of enjoyable activities should be used to accommodate diverse populations.
2) It needs to be accepted that, as a professional, I have good reason to assign the work that I do.
3) Learners should know how useful and beneficial the learning opportunities I provide them with are.
4) If they lack educational value and real-world relevance, they are not maximizing the educational experience.
5) Every planned academic task should work to perfect competency in the uses and benefits of a content.

My Attitude About Assessment Scores And Grades Is This:
1) They do not define you, nor should they jeopardize self-esteem, mental health, or future prospects.
2) If work is completed, and the instructions are followed, a respectable grade should always be manageable.
3) They are a validation of effort spent and the learning which occurred while pursuing an education.
4) They should represent the appraised value of learning completed and education attained.
5) They must confirm proficiency, affirm mastery, and expose lapses in an educational pursuit, qualitatively.

My Attitude About The Young People Who Attend School Is This:
1) I want them to know how special, capable, and deserving of love they are.
2) There is so much they do not know, so much they need to learn.
3) Quality space and opportunity to pursue an education is what they need to prepare for the future.
4) Success and fulfillment in life are possible if I can assist them in maximizing their educational experience.
5) Discovering and unlocking their true potential and gifts will take more work than they could ever imagine.

My Attitude About Social Interactions And Extracurricular Activities Is This:
1) They are highly important as they allow for connectedness and social-emotional development.
2) Their contribution to building and promoting school culture is unlike anything else a school has to offer.
3) They are useful and beneficial, giving them educational value.
4) Using these mediums to teach lessons and provide experience can have high-quality educational benefits.
5) If they complement an educational pursuit, I support them. If they detract from it, they should be given up.

5-9	10-14	15-19	20-24	25
Caregiver	Teacher	Educator	Profound Mentor	Intense Trainer

EDUCATIONAL PURSUIT EVALUATION

An education is a unique assortment of information that one can possess (1), understand (2), know how to use (3), and benefit from (4). Thus, despite effort, intention, or desire, an individual's inability to acquire any prerequisite component of an education prevents them from acquiring a complete education. As learning is facilitated, and assessments are observed, learners should possess qualitative evidence revealing an educational pursuit accounting for more than a collection of completed tasks and isolated/disconnected information. This rubric contains one single scale with all criteria to be included in the evaluation being considered simultaneously. Subsequently, a single score is given to that graded work based on an overall judgement of the demonstration.

Range: 90 -100% 5) Success: "I Am Educated"	Grade: A	Demonstration revealing qualitative evidence of a learner's mastery of Educational Value Continuum™ elements. Through skillful explanation, exhibition, or presentation of evidence, learner has proven themselves to be qualified and likely to attain real-world success stemming from the *Minimum Functionality* and *Maximum Possibility* learner statements they express with confidence.
Range: 80-89% 4) Value: "I Benefit From It"	Grade: B	Demonstration revealing qualitative evidence of a learner's proficiency with Educational Value Continuum™ elements. Through skillful explanation, exhibition, or presentation of evidence, learner has proven they are qualified to make *Maximum Possibility* learner statements with confidence.
Range: 70-79% 3) Competence: "I Can Use It"	Grade: C	Demonstration revealing qualitative evidence of a learner's proficiency with Educational Value Continuum™ elements. Through skillful explanation, exhibition, or presentation of evidence, learner has proven they are qualified to make *Minimum Functionality* learner statements with confidence.
Range: 60-69% 2) Understanding: "I Get It"	Grade: D	Demonstration revealing comprehension of basic facts and general information possessed, allowing the relevance, significance, and necessity of the content being taught to be understood. Subsequently, the learner's understanding forecasts probable achievement with the functions and possibilities of the content.
Range: 25-59% 1) Possession: "I Know It"	Grade: F	Demonstration revealing acquisition of basic facts and general information that is pertinent to knowing about and grasping subject material in a fundamental way. Comprehension and informational grounding, if any exists, are ambiguous, unsubstantial, and illogical. While knowledge is possessed, learner is void of understanding, use, and benefit from the content.
Range: 0-24% 0) Uneducated: "I Don't Know"	Grade: I or N/A	Demonstration revealing a lack of basic content knowledge. It is evident and clear that no sincere effort was put forth to pursue, let alone acquire, an education. While *some* information may be known, and possibly even understood (quantifiably), the qualitative nature of this demonstration is indicative of a desperate attempt to salvage points.

EDUCATIONAL PURSUIT EVALUATION

Criterion	SUCCESS (5)	VALUE (4)	COMPETENCE (3)	UNDERSTANDING (2)	POSSESSION (1)
Compliance: Did You Listen? To what level or magnitude does it appear directions and guidelines were followed appropriately?	Instructions were followed precisely, allowing no room for missteps, mistakes, or oversights to occur.	Instructions were carefully followed, leaving little to no room for missteps, mistakes, or oversights to occur.	Instructions were mostly followed, allowing few missteps, mistakes, or oversights to occur.	Instructions were partially followed, causing multiple missteps, mistakes, and oversights to occur.	Instructions were hardly followed, causing abundant missteps, mistakes, and oversights to occur.
Curiosity: Did You Ask Questions? What attempts were made to attain greater clarity and comprehension or uncover an elevated level of appeal for the task?	Insight was sought after to gain understanding that would cause the likelihood of real-world success from implemented learning to increase.	Insight was sought after in an effort to gain understanding that would cause the likelihood of benefitting from learning to increase.	Insight was sought after in an effort to gain understanding that would cause the likelihood of using information from learning to increase.	Little insight was sought after, and minimal understanding was gained past that which the instructor provided freely.	No insight was sought after, nor was any understanding gained past that which was voluntarily provided by the instructor.
Participation: Did You Work? To what level or magnitude does it appear that the energy, activity, and focus of the student were purposed for educational achievement?	Deeply determined while eagerly and expectantly working to maximize the real-world possibilities of the educational experience.	Focused energy and optimism while working to pursue an education with more real-world implications than academic attainment or achievement.	Sincere and attentive while being effectively involved in the learning process.	Slight disinterest and/or carelessness were shown but gaining understanding did appear to be the purpose of learning.	Disinterest and carelessness were present in abundance as work appeared to be for the purpose of compliance and completion.
Sincere Effort: Did You Try? To what level or magnitude does it appear that full capability is the actual occurrence of the educational pursuit taking place?	Empirical evidence suggests the energy exerted on the educational pursuit is fully maximized considering physical and intellectual capability.	Empirical evidence suggests the energy exerted on the educational pursuit is enhanced considering physical and intellectual capability.	Empirical evidence suggests the energy exerted on the educational pursuit is on par with what physical and intellectual capability would allow.	Empirical evidence suggests the energy exerted on the educational pursuit is less than that which physical and intellectual capability would allow.	Empirical evidence suggests the energy exerted on the education pursuit is well below that which physical and intellectual capability would allow.
Quality & Style: Did You Care? What concentration of personal artistry, interest, talent, or craftsmanship was adapted and integrated into the demonstration?	Work appears to have been edited, revamped, and polished critically, resembling great honor was taken in accomplishing it.	Work appears to have been edited, revamped, and polished well, resembling a sense of personal pride was taken in completing it.	Work appears to be edited, revamped, and polished, resembling satisfaction was attained in completing it.	Work appears to have been slightly edited, revamped, or polished, resembling some level of care.	Work does not appear to have been edited, revamped, or polished past one primary attempt at completion.
Educational Achievement: Are You Educated? What educational acquirement is your demonstration an accomplishment of?	Proficient explanation, exhibition, or presentation that reveals evidence of real-world success capabilities.	Proficient explanation, exhibition, or presentation that parallels and resembles evidence of benefit.	Proficient explanation, exhibition, or presentation revealing possession of knowledge and/or ability of use.	Proficient explanation, exhibition, or presentation revealing possession of content understanding.	Proficient explanation, exhibition, or presentation revealing possession of basic content knowledge.

EDUCATIONAL PROVISION EVALUATION

An education is a unique assortment of information that one can possess (1), understand (2), know how to use (3), and benefit from (4). Thus, despite effort, intention, or desire, an instructor's ability to, intentionally, teach lessons and plan activities that allow students to be exposed to, explore, and experience an education allows the pursuit of a complete education to occur efficiently. As teaching and learning commence, an instructor should have qualitative evidence revealing their facilitation of an educational experience has accounted for more than a collection of completed tasks and isolated/disconnected information. This rubric contains one single scale with all criteria to be included in the evaluation being considered simultaneously. Subsequently, a single score is given to that observation based on an overall judgement of the instructional attempt.

Range: 90 -100% Grade: A	5) Success: "I Educate Them"	Instruction revealing qualitative evidence that an instructor has facilitated an educational experience centered around mastery of Educational Value Continuum™ elements. By skillfully leading, provoking, and supporting learners through the educational process, the probability of a learner expressing *Minimum Functionality* and *Maximum Possibility* learner statements with confidence, and attaining real-world success, is raised exponentially.
Range: 80-89% Grade: B	4) Value: "I Benefit Them"	Instruction revealing qualitative evidence that an instructor has facilitated an educational experience centered around proficiency in Educational Value Continuum™ elements. By skillfully leading, provoking, and supporting learners through the educational process, the probability of a learner expressing *Maximum Possibility* learner statements with confidence is raised exponentially.
Range: 70-79% Grade: C	3) Competence: "I Equip Them"	Instruction revealing qualitative evidence that an instructor has facilitated an educational experience centered around proficiency in Educational Value Continuum™ elements. By skillfully leading, provoking, and supporting learners through the educational process, the probability of a learner expressing *Minimum Functionality* learner statements with confidence is raised exponentially.
Range: 60-69% Grade: D	2) Understanding: "I Enlighten Them"	Instruction revealing qualitative evidence that an instructor has facilitated an educational experience centered around comprehension of basic facts and general information possessed. This experience allows the relevance, significance, and necessity of content being taught to be understood. Subsequently, instruction forecasts probable provision of learning opportunities with the functions and possibilities of the content.
Range: 25-59% Grade: F	1) Possession: "I Inform Them"	Instruction revealing qualitative evidence that an instructor has facilitated an educational experience centered around acquisition of basic facts and general information that is pertinent to knowing about and grasping subject material in a fundamental way. Comprehension and informational grounding are likely to be ambiguous, unsubstantial, and incoherent. While content is covered, learners are deprived of understanding, use, and benefit.
Range: 0-24% Grade: I or N/A	0) Uneducated: "I Don't Know"	Instruction revealing qualitative evidence that an instructor has facilitated an educational experience lacking basic content knowledge. It is evident and clear that no sincere effort was put forth to lead, provoke, or support an educational pursuit. While *some* content may have been covered, the qualitative nature of this experience is grossly negligent.

EDUCATIONAL PROVISION EVALUATION

Criteria	POSSESSION (1)	UNDERSTANDING (2)	COMPETENCE (3)	VALUE (4)	SUCCESS (5)
Guidance: Did You Lead? To what level or magnitude does it appear directions and guidelines were explained and broken down?	Instructions were implied and/or lacking, causing abundant missteps, mistakes, and oversights to occur.	Instructions were vague, causing multiple missteps, mistakes, and oversights to occur.	Instructions were clear but not thoroughly explained, allowing missteps, mistakes, and/or oversights to occur.	Instructions were carefully explained, leaving little to no room for missteps, mistakes, or oversights to occur.	Instructions were laid out with precision, allowing no room for missteps, mistakes, or oversights to occur.
Engagement: Did You Provoke? What attempts were made to inspire greater inquiry and investigation or to bring an elevated level of interest to the lesson?	Instructor expected the interests of learners to be sparked simply by presenting material and exposing them to content.	Instructor sought to spark the interests of learners by providing them with an understanding of presented materials and content alone.	Instructor sought to prompt learners and spark their interests by providing them with an understanding of how content from the lesson can be useful.	Instructor sought to provide an understanding of how the lesson's content could likely benefit learners to prompt them and spark their interests.	Instructor sought to provide an understanding of how the lesson could increase the likelihood of real-world success to prompt and spark the interests of learners.
Management: Did You Support? To what level or magnitude was instruction aimed at completing the educational process and providing a complete educational experience?	Indifference and neglect toward the educational value of the lesson's content were prevalent as instruction appeared to accomplish nothing more than the completion of the lesson.	Slight indifference and/or neglect were shown toward the educational value of the lesson's content, but instruction did appear to fulfill the basic requirements of teaching.	Careful to lead learners through the complete educational process and provide them with a quality educational experience.	Careful and practical in leading learners through the complete educational process and placing their focus on success that is greater than academic achievement.	Meticulous and proficient in leading learners through the complete educational process and maximizing the probability of real-world success.
Sincere Effort: Did You Try? To what level or magnitude does it appear that the instructor's full capabilities were utilized to stimulate learning?	Empirical evidence suggests the energy exerted while facilitating the educational experience is well below that which physical and intellectual capability would allow.	Empirical evidence suggests the energy exerted while facilitating the educational experience is less than that which physical and intellectual capability would allow.	Empirical evidence suggests the energy exerted while facilitating the educational experience is on par with what physical and intellectual capability would allow.	Empirical evidence suggests the energy exerted while facilitating the educational experience is enhanced considering physical and intellectual capability.	Empirical evidence suggests the energy exerted while facilitating the educational experience is fully maximized considering physical and intellectual capability.
Quality & Style: Did You Care? What concentration of personal artistry, interest, talent, or craftsmanship was adapted and integrated into instruction?	Lesson does not appear to have been adjusted, updated, or polished past one primary attempt to design it.	Lesson appears to have been slightly adjusted, updated, and/or polished, showing some level of care for the design and presentation of it.	Lesson appears to have been adjusted, updated, and/or polished, implying satisfaction was attained in designing and presenting it.	Lesson appears to have been adjusted, updated, and/or polished well, implying a sense of personal pride was taken in designing and presenting it.	Lesson appears to have been adjusted, updated, and/or polished critically, implying great honor was taken in designing and presenting it.
Experience Facilitated: Are You Educating? Was exposure to, exploration of, and experience with an education the collective purpose of instruction?	Leading, provoking, and supporting learners has provided them space and opportunity to possess basic content knowledge.	Leading, provoking, and supporting learners has provided them space and opportunity to possess an understanding of content.	Proficient leading, provoking, and supporting of learners has provided them space and opportunity to pursue and acquire a quality education.	High-quality leading, provoking, and supporting of learners has elevated probable success passed academic achievement.	Superior leading, provoking, and supporting of learners has maximized the possibility of real-world success.

EDUCATION RECEIPT

Academic Audit:

Having each of these four components (possession, understanding, knowledge of use, and evidence of benefit) for a unique assortment of information is what it means to be educated. Anything short of the attainment of these four components is not an education. When you go through a lesson, are you clear on what component of an education that lesson is contributing to? Allow your students to attain that same clarity with this certificate by confirming their learning is, indeed, educational.

1) POSSESSESSION:
What information do you now have?

_____
_____
_____
_____
_____
_____
_____
_____
_____
_____
_____

2) UNDERSTANDING:
How is it understood, in practical terms, by you?

_____
_____
_____
_____
_____
_____
_____
_____
_____
_____
_____

EVC Minimum(s):_____
_____
EVC Maximum(s):_____
_____

3) KNOWLEDGE OF USE:
What can you actually *do* with it in the real-world?

_____
_____
_____
_____
_____
_____
_____
_____
_____

4) EVIDENCE OF BENEFIT:
Likely/potential outcome(s) from using it that way?

_____
_____
_____
_____
_____
_____
_____
_____
_____

COURSE

SCHOOL YEAR
20 ___ / ___ 20

UNIT SCHEDULE

UNIT TITLE	PROJECTED TIMELINE	TIME SPENT

DESIGN IT
AM I LEADING, PROVOKING, AND SUPPORTING AN EDUCATIONAL PURSUIT?

Standard: _____

Content: _____

Designation: _____

EVC Minimum:
_____
_____
_____

EVC Maximum:
_____
_____
_____

EXPOSE Them To It

Let Them EXPLORE It

Activities:
_____
_____

Strategies:
_____
_____

Materials:
_____
_____

Knowledge & Competence:
_____
_____

Assignments / Assessments / EVC Statements:
_____
_____
_____

Once They **EXPERIENCE** It

They Will ENGAGE In

Necessary Activity:
Think / Do
See / Listen

Likely Questions:
_____
_____
_____

Likely Difficulty:
_____
_____

Cultural:
_____
_____

Developmental:
_____
_____

Individual:
_____
_____

That Which **EXCITES** Them

Standard: _____

Content: _____

Designation: _____

EVC Minimum:
_____
_____
_____

EVC Maximum:
_____
_____
_____

EXPOSE Them To It

Let Them EXPLORE It

Activities:
_____
_____

Strategies:
_____
_____

Materials:
_____
_____

Knowledge & Competence:
_____
_____

Assignments / Assessments / EVC Statements:
_____
_____
_____

Once They **EXPERIENCE** It

They Will ENGAGE In

Necessary Activity:
Think / Do
See / Listen

Likely Questions:
_____
_____
_____

Likely Difficulty:
_____
_____

Cultural:
_____
_____

Developmental:
_____
_____

Individual:
_____
_____

That Which **EXCITES** Them

Instructional Level: Caregiver   /   Teacher   /   Educator   /   Profound Mentor   /   Intense Trainer

DESIGN IT

DID I FACILITATE THE EDUCATIONAL PROCESS AND FULFILL THE MISSION OF EDUCATION?

Unit: _____

Week Of: _____

Standard: _____

Content: _____

Designation: _____

EVC Minimum:
_____
_____
_____
_____

EVC Maximum:
_____
_____
_____
_____

EXPOSE Them To It

Let Them EXPLORE It

Activities:
_____
_____

Strategies:
_____
_____

Materials:
_____
_____
_____

Knowledge & Competence:
_____
_____
_____

Assignments / Assessments / EVC Statements:
_____
_____
_____
_____

Once They EXPERIENCE It

They Will ENGAGE In

Necessary Activity:
Think / Do
See / Listen

Likely Questions:
_____
_____

Likely Difficulty:
_____
_____
_____
_____

Cultural:
_____
_____

Developmental:
_____
_____

Individual:
_____
_____
_____

That Which EXCITES Them

Standard: _____

Content: _____

Designation: _____

EVC Minimum:
_____
_____
_____
_____

EVC Maximum:
_____
_____
_____
_____

EXPOSE Them To It

Let Them EXPLORE It

Activities:
_____
_____

Strategies:
_____
_____

Materials:
_____
_____
_____

Knowledge & Competence:
_____
_____
_____

Assignments / Assessments / EVC Statements:
_____
_____
_____
_____

Once They EXPERIENCE It

They Will ENGAGE In

Necessary Activity:
Think / Do
See / Listen

Likely Questions:
_____
_____

Likely Difficulty:
_____
_____
_____
_____

Cultural:
_____
_____

Developmental:
_____
_____

Individual:
_____
_____
_____

That Which EXCITES Them

Educational Provision: Possession / Understanding / Competence / Value / Success

DESIGN IT
AM I LEADING, PROVOKING, AND SUPPORTING AN EDUCATIONAL PURSUIT?

Standard: _____

Content: _____

Designation: _____

EVC Minimum:
_____
_____
_____

EVC Maximum:
_____
_____
_____
_____

EXPOSE Them To It

Let Them EXPLORE It

Activities:
_____
_____

Strategies:
_____
_____

Materials:
_____
_____

Knowledge & Competence:
_____
_____

Assignments / Assessments / EVC Statements:
_____
_____
_____

Once They EXPERIENCE It

They Will ENGAGE In

Necessary Activity:
Think / Do
See / Listen

Likely Questions:
_____
_____
_____

Likely Difficulty:
_____
_____

Cultural:
_____
_____

Developmental:
_____
_____

Individual:
_____
_____

That Which EXCITES Them

Standard: _____

Content: _____

Designation: _____

EVC Minimum:
_____
_____
_____

EVC Maximum:
_____
_____
_____
_____

EXPOSE Them To It

Let Them EXPLORE It

Activities:
_____
_____

Strategies:
_____
_____

Materials:
_____
_____

Knowledge & Competence:
_____
_____

Assignments / Assessments / EVC Statements:
_____
_____
_____

Once They EXPERIENCE It

They Will ENGAGE In

Necessary Activity:
Think / Do
See / Listen

Likely Questions:
_____
_____
_____

Likely Difficulty:
_____
_____

Cultural:
_____
_____

Developmental:
_____
_____

Individual:
_____
_____

That Which EXCITES Them

Instructional Level: Caregiver / Teacher / Educator / Profound Mentor / Intense Trainer

DESIGN IT

DID I FACILITATE THE EDUCATIONAL PROCESS AND FULFILL THE MISSION OF EDUCATION?

Unit: _____

Week Of: _____

Standard: _____

Content: _____

Designation: _____

EVC Minimum:	**Let Them EXPLORE It**	Knowledge & Competence:	**They Will ENGAGE In**	Cultural:
_____	Activities:	_____	**Necessary Activity:** Think / Do See / Listen	_____
_____	_____	_____	**Likely Questions:**	_____
EVC Maximum:	Strategies:	Assignments / Assessments / EVC Statements:	_____	Developmental:
_____	Materials:	_____	**Likely Difficulty:**	Individual:
EXPOSE Them To It		**Once They EXPERIENCE It**		**That Which EXCITES Them**

Standard: _____

Content: _____

Designation: _____

EVC Minimum:	**Let Them EXPLORE It**	Knowledge & Competence:	**They Will ENGAGE In**	Cultural:
_____	Activities:	_____	**Necessary Activity:** Think / Do See / Listen	_____
_____	_____	_____	**Likely Questions:**	_____
EVC Maximum:	Strategies:	Assignments / Assessments / EVC Statements:	_____	Developmental:
_____	Materials:	_____	**Likely Difficulty:**	Individual:
EXPOSE Them To It		**Once They EXPERIENCE It**		**That Which EXCITES Them**

Educational Provision: Possession / Understanding / Competence / Value / Success

DESIGN IT
AM I LEADING, PROVOKING, AND SUPPORTING AN EDUCATIONAL PURSUIT?

Standard: _____

Content: _____

Designation: _____

EVC Minimum:
_____
_____
_____

EVC Maximum:
_____
_____
_____
_____

EXPOSE Them To It

Let Them EXPLORE It

Activities:
_____
_____

Strategies:
_____
_____

Materials:
_____
_____

Knowledge & Competence:
_____
_____

Assignments / Assessments / EVC Statements:
_____
_____
_____

Once They **EXPERIENCE** It

They Will ENGAGE In

Necessary Activity:
Think / Do
See / Listen

Likely Questions:
_____
_____
_____

Likely Difficulty:
_____
_____
_____

Cultural:
_____
_____

Developmental:
_____
_____

Individual:
_____
_____

That Which **EXCITES** Them

Standard: _____

Content: _____

Designation: _____

EVC Minimum:
_____
_____
_____

EVC Maximum:
_____
_____
_____
_____

EXPOSE Them To It

Let Them EXPLORE It

Activities:
_____
_____

Strategies:
_____
_____

Materials:
_____
_____

Knowledge & Competence:
_____
_____

Assignments / Assessments / EVC Statements:
_____
_____
_____

Once They **EXPERIENCE** It

They Will ENGAGE In

Necessary Activity:
Think / Do
See / Listen

Likely Questions:
_____
_____
_____

Likely Difficulty:
_____
_____
_____

Cultural:
_____
_____

Developmental:
_____
_____

Individual:
_____
_____

That Which **EXCITES** Them

Instructional Level: Caregiver / Teacher / Educator / Profound Mentor / Intense Trainer

DESIGN IT
DID I FACILITATE THE EDUCATIONAL PROCESS AND FULFILL THE MISSION OF EDUCATION?

Unit: _____

Week Of: _____

Standard: _____

Content: _____

Designation: _____

EVC Minimum:	**Let Them EXPLORE It**		**They Will ENGAGE In**	
	Activities:	Knowledge & Competence:	Necessary Activity: Think / Do See / Listen	Cultural:
			Likely Questions:	
EVC Maximum:	Strategies:	Assignments / Assessments / EVC Statements:		Developmental:
	Materials:		Likely Difficulty:	Individual:
EXPOSE Them To It		**Once They EXPERIENCE It**		**That Which EXCITES Them**

Standard: _____

Content: _____

Designation: _____

EVC Minimum:	**Let Them EXPLORE It**		**They Will ENGAGE In**	
	Activities:	Knowledge & Competence:	Necessary Activity: Think / Do See / Listen	Cultural:
			Likely Questions:	
EVC Maximum:	Strategies:	Assignments / Assessments / EVC Statements:		Developmental:
	Materials:		Likely Difficulty:	Individual:
EXPOSE Them To It		**Once They EXPERIENCE It**		**That Which EXCITES Them**

Educational Provision: Possession   /   Understanding   /   Competence   /   Value   /   Success

DESIGN IT
AM I LEADING, PROVOKING, AND SUPPORTING AN EDUCATIONAL PURSUIT?

Standard: _____

Content: _____

Designation: _____

EVC Minimum:
_____
_____
_____

EVC Maximum:
_____
_____
_____

EXPOSE Them To It

Let Them EXPLORE It

Activities:
_____
_____

Strategies:
_____
_____

Materials:
_____
_____

Knowledge & Competence:
_____
_____

Assignments / Assessments / EVC Statements:
_____
_____

Once They **EXPERIENCE** It

They Will ENGAGE In

Necessary Activity:
Think / Do
See / Listen

Likely Questions:
_____
_____

Likely Difficulty:
_____
_____

Cultural:
_____
_____

Developmental:
_____
_____

Individual:
_____
_____

That Which **EXCITES** Them

Standard: _____

Content: _____

Designation: _____

EVC Minimum:
_____
_____
_____

EVC Maximum:
_____
_____
_____

EXPOSE Them To It

Let Them EXPLORE It

Activities:
_____
_____

Strategies:
_____
_____

Materials:
_____
_____

Knowledge & Competence:
_____
_____

Assignments / Assessments / EVC Statements:
_____
_____

Once They **EXPERIENCE** It

They Will ENGAGE In

Necessary Activity:
Think / Do
See / Listen

Likely Questions:
_____
_____

Likely Difficulty:
_____
_____

Cultural:
_____
_____

Developmental:
_____
_____

Individual:
_____
_____

That Which **EXCITES** Them

Instructional Level: Caregiver   /   Teacher   /   Educator   /   Profound Mentor   /   Intense Trainer

DESIGN IT
DID I FACILITATE THE EDUCATIONAL PROCESS AND FULFILL THE MISSION OF EDUCATION?

Unit: _____

Week Of: _____

Standard: _____

Content: _____

Designation: _____

EVC Minimum:

_____

_____

_____

EVC Maximum:

_____

_____

_____

EXPOSE Them To It

Let Them EXPLORE It

Activities:

_____

_____

Strategies:

_____

_____

Materials:

_____

_____

Knowledge & Competence:

_____

_____

Assignments / Assessments / EVC Statements:

_____

_____

_____

Once They EXPERIENCE It

They Will ENGAGE In

Necessary Activity:
Think / Do
See / Listen

Likely Questions:

_____

_____

_____

Likely Difficulty:

_____

_____

Cultural:

_____

_____

Developmental:

_____

_____

Individual:

_____

_____

That Which EXCITES Them

Standard: _____

Content: _____

Designation: _____

EVC Minimum:

_____

_____

_____

EVC Maximum:

_____

_____

_____

EXPOSE Them To It

Let Them EXPLORE It

Activities:

_____

_____

Strategies:

_____

_____

Materials:

_____

_____

Knowledge & Competence:

_____

_____

Assignments / Assessments / EVC Statements:

_____

_____

_____

Once They EXPERIENCE It

They Will ENGAGE In

Necessary Activity:
Think / Do
See / Listen

Likely Questions:

_____

_____

_____

Likely Difficulty:

_____

_____

Cultural:

_____

_____

Developmental:

_____

_____

Individual:

_____

_____

That Which EXCITES Them

Educational Provision: Possession / Understanding / Competence / Value / Success

DESIGN IT
AM I LEADING, PROVOKING, AND SUPPORTING AN EDUCATIONAL PURSUIT?

Standard: _____

Content: _____

Designation: _____

EVC Minimum:
_____
_____
_____
_____

EVC Maximum:
_____
_____
_____
_____

EXPOSE Them To It

Let Them EXPLORE It

Activities:
_____
_____

Strategies:
_____
_____

Materials:
_____
_____

Knowledge & Competence:
_____
_____

Assignments / Assessments / EVC Statements:
_____
_____
_____

Once They **EXPERIENCE** It

They Will ENGAGE In

Necessary Activity:
Think / Do
See / Listen

Likely Questions:
_____
_____
_____

Likely Difficulty:
_____
_____

Cultural:
_____
_____

Developmental:
_____
_____

Individual:
_____
_____

That Which **EXCITES** Them

Standard: _____

Content: _____

Designation: _____

EVC Minimum:
_____
_____
_____
_____

EVC Maximum:
_____
_____
_____
_____

EXPOSE Them To It

Let Them EXPLORE It

Activities:
_____
_____

Strategies:
_____
_____

Materials:
_____
_____

Knowledge & Competence:
_____
_____

Assignments / Assessments / EVC Statements:
_____
_____
_____

Once They **EXPERIENCE** It

They Will ENGAGE In

Necessary Activity:
Think / Do
See / Listen

Likely Questions:
_____
_____
_____

Likely Difficulty:
_____
_____

Cultural:
_____
_____

Developmental:
_____
_____

Individual:
_____
_____

That Which **EXCITES** Them

Instructional Level: Caregiver / Teacher / Educator / Profound Mentor / Intense Trainer

DESIGN IT
Did I Facilitate The Educational Process And Fulfill The Mission Of Education?

Unit: _____

Week Of: _____

Standard: _____

Content: _____

Designation: _____

EXPOSE Them To It

EVC Minimum:
_____
_____
_____
_____

EVC Maximum:
_____
_____
_____
_____

Let Them EXPLORE It

Activities:
_____
_____
_____

Strategies:
_____
_____

Materials:
_____
_____
_____

Once They EXPERIENCE It

Knowledge & Competence:
_____
_____

Assignments / Assessments / EVC Statements:
_____
_____
_____
_____

They Will ENGAGE In

Necessary Activity:
Think / Do
See / Listen

Likely Questions:
_____
_____
_____

Likely Difficulty:
_____
_____
_____

That Which EXCITES Them

Cultural:
_____
_____
_____

Developmental:
_____
_____

Individual:
_____
_____

Standard: _____

Content: _____

Designation: _____

EXPOSE Them To It

EVC Minimum:
_____
_____
_____
_____

EVC Maximum:
_____
_____
_____
_____

Let Them EXPLORE It

Activities:
_____
_____
_____

Strategies:
_____
_____

Materials:
_____
_____
_____

Once They EXPERIENCE It

Knowledge & Competence:
_____
_____

Assignments / Assessments / EVC Statements:
_____
_____
_____
_____

They Will ENGAGE In

Necessary Activity:
Think / Do
See / Listen

Likely Questions:
_____
_____
_____

Likely Difficulty:
_____
_____
_____

That Which EXCITES Them

Cultural:
_____
_____
_____

Developmental:
_____
_____

Individual:
_____
_____

Educational Provision: Possession / Understanding / Competence / Value / Success

DESIGN IT
AM I LEADING, PROVOKING, AND SUPPORTING AN EDUCATIONAL PURSUIT?

Standard: _____

Content: _____

Designation: _____

EVC Minimum:
_____
_____
_____
_____

EVC Maximum:
_____
_____
_____
_____

EXPOSE Them To It

Let Them EXPLORE It

Activities:
_____
_____

Strategies:
_____
_____

Materials:
_____
_____

Knowledge & Competence:
_____
_____

Assignments / Assessments / EVC Statements:
_____
_____
_____

Once They EXPERIENCE It

They Will ENGAGE In

Necessary Activity:
Think / Do
See / Listen

Likely Questions:
_____
_____
_____

Likely Difficulty:
_____
_____
_____

Cultural:
_____
_____

Developmental:
_____
_____

Individual:
_____
_____

That Which EXCITES Them

Standard: _____

Content: _____

Designation: _____

EVC Minimum:
_____
_____
_____
_____

EVC Maximum:
_____
_____
_____
_____

EXPOSE Them To It

Let Them EXPLORE It

Activities:
_____
_____

Strategies:
_____
_____

Materials:
_____
_____

Knowledge & Competence:
_____
_____

Assignments / Assessments / EVC Statements:
_____
_____
_____

Once They EXPERIENCE It

They Will ENGAGE In

Necessary Activity:
Think / Do
See / Listen

Likely Questions:
_____
_____
_____

Likely Difficulty:
_____
_____
_____

Cultural:
_____
_____

Developmental:
_____
_____

Individual:
_____
_____

That Which EXCITES Them

Instructional Level: Caregiver / Teacher / Educator / Profound Mentor / Intense Trainer

DESIGN IT
Did I Facilitate The Educational Process And Fulfill The Mission Of Education?

Unit: _____

Week Of: _____

Standard: _____

Content: _____

Designation: _____

EVC Minimum:
_____
_____
_____
_____

EVC Maximum:
_____
_____
_____
_____

EXPOSE Them To It

Let Them EXPLORE It

Activities:
_____
_____

Strategies:
_____
_____

Materials:
_____
_____
_____

Knowledge & Competence:
_____
_____
_____

Assignments / Assessments / EVC Statements:
_____
_____
_____
_____

Once They EXPERIENCE It

They Will ENGAGE In

Necessary Activity:
Think / Do
See / Listen

Likely Questions:
_____
_____
_____

Likely Difficulty:
_____
_____
_____
_____

Cultural:
_____
_____
_____

Developmental:
_____
_____

Individual:
_____
_____

That Which EXCITES Them

Standard: _____

Content: _____

Designation: _____

EVC Minimum:
_____
_____
_____
_____

EVC Maximum:
_____
_____
_____
_____

EXPOSE Them To It

Let Them EXPLORE It

Activities:
_____
_____

Strategies:
_____
_____

Materials:
_____
_____
_____

Knowledge & Competence:
_____
_____
_____

Assignments / Assessments / EVC Statements:
_____
_____
_____
_____

Once They EXPERIENCE It

They Will ENGAGE In

Necessary Activity:
Think / Do
See / Listen

Likely Questions:
_____
_____
_____

Likely Difficulty:
_____
_____
_____
_____

Cultural:
_____
_____
_____

Developmental:
_____
_____

Individual:
_____
_____

That Which EXCITES Them

Educational Provision: Possession / Understanding / Competence / Value / Success

DESIGN IT
AM I LEADING, PROVOKING, AND SUPPORTING AN EDUCATIONAL PURSUIT?

Standard: _____

Content: _____

Designation: _____

EVC Minimum:
_____
_____
_____
_____

EVC Maximum:
_____
_____
_____
_____

EXPOSE Them To It

Let Them EXPLORE It

Activities:
_____
_____

Strategies:
_____
_____

Materials:
_____
_____
_____

Knowledge & Competence:
_____
_____
_____

Assignments / Assessments / EVC Statements:
_____
_____
_____
_____

Once They **EXPERIENCE** It

They Will ENGAGE In

Necessary Activity:
Think / Do
See / Listen

Likely Questions:
_____
_____
_____

Likely Difficulty:
_____
_____
_____

Cultural:
_____
_____

Developmental:
_____
_____

Individual:
_____
_____
_____

That Which **EXCITES** Them

Standard: _____

Content: _____

Designation: _____

EVC Minimum:
_____
_____
_____
_____

EVC Maximum:
_____
_____
_____
_____

EXPOSE Them To It

Let Them EXPLORE It

Activities:
_____
_____

Strategies:
_____
_____

Materials:
_____
_____
_____

Knowledge & Competence:
_____
_____
_____

Assignments / Assessments / EVC Statements:
_____
_____
_____
_____

Once They **EXPERIENCE** It

They Will ENGAGE In

Necessary Activity:
Think / Do
See / Listen

Likely Questions:
_____
_____
_____

Likely Difficulty:
_____
_____
_____

Cultural:
_____
_____

Developmental:
_____
_____

Individual:
_____
_____
_____

That Which **EXCITES** Them

Instructional Level: Caregiver / Teacher / Educator / Profound Mentor / Intense Trainer

DESIGN IT

DID I FACILITATE THE EDUCATIONAL PROCESS AND FULFILL THE MISSION OF EDUCATION?

Unit: _____

Week Of: _____

Standard: _____

Content: _____

Designation: _____

EVC Minimum:
_____
_____
_____
_____

EVC Maximum:
_____
_____
_____
_____

EXPOSE Them To It

Let Them EXPLORE It

Activities:
_____
_____

Strategies:
_____
_____

Materials:
_____
_____
_____

Knowledge & Competence:
_____
_____

Assignments / Assessments / EVC Statements:
_____
_____
_____
_____

Once They EXPERIENCE It

They Will ENGAGE In

Necessary Activity:
Think / Do
See / Listen

Likely Questions:
_____
_____
_____

Likely Difficulty:
_____
_____
_____

Cultural:
_____
_____

Developmental:
_____
_____

Individual:
_____
_____
_____

That Which EXCITES Them

Standard: _____

Content: _____

Designation: _____

EVC Minimum:
_____
_____
_____
_____

EVC Maximum:
_____
_____
_____
_____

EXPOSE Them To It

Let Them EXPLORE It

Activities:
_____
_____

Strategies:
_____
_____

Materials:
_____
_____
_____

Knowledge & Competence:
_____
_____

Assignments / Assessments / EVC Statements:
_____
_____
_____
_____

Once They EXPERIENCE It

They Will ENGAGE In

Necessary Activity:
Think / Do
See / Listen

Likely Questions:
_____
_____
_____

Likely Difficulty:
_____
_____
_____

Cultural:
_____
_____

Developmental:
_____
_____

Individual:
_____
_____
_____

That Which EXCITES Them

Educational Provision: Possession / Understanding / Competence / Value / Success

DESIGN IT
AM I LEADING, PROVOKING, AND SUPPORTING AN EDUCATIONAL PURSUIT?

Standard: _____

Content: _____

Designation: _____

Let Them EXPLORE It

They Will ENGAGE In

EVC Minimum:	Activities:	Knowledge & Competence:	Necessary Activity: Think / Do See / Listen	Cultural:
_____	_____	_____		_____
_____	_____	_____	Likely Questions:	_____
_____	Strategies:	_____	_____	Developmental:
EVC Maximum:	_____	Assignments / Assessments / EVC Statements:	_____	_____
_____	Materials:	_____	Likely Difficulty:	Individual:
_____	_____	_____	_____	_____

EXPOSE Them To It

Once They EXPERIENCE It

That Which EXCITES Them

Standard: _____

Content: _____

Designation: _____

Let Them EXPLORE It

They Will ENGAGE In

EVC Minimum:	Activities:	Knowledge & Competence:	Necessary Activity: Think / Do See / Listen	Cultural:
_____	_____	_____		_____
_____	_____	_____	Likely Questions:	_____
_____	Strategies:	_____	_____	Developmental:
EVC Maximum:	_____	Assignments / Assessments / EVC Statements:	_____	_____
_____	Materials:	_____	Likely Difficulty:	Individual:
_____	_____	_____	_____	_____

EXPOSE Them To It

Once They EXPERIENCE It

That Which EXCITES Them

Instructional Level: Caregiver / Teacher / Educator / Profound Mentor / Intense Trainer

DESIGN IT
DID I FACILITATE THE EDUCATIONAL PROCESS AND
FULFILL THE MISSION OF EDUCATION?

Unit: _____

Week Of: _____

Standard: _____

Content: _____

Designation: _____

EVC Minimum:
_____
_____
_____
_____

EVC Maximum:
_____
_____
_____
_____

EXPOSE Them To It

Let Them EXPLORE It

Activities:
_____
_____

Strategies:
_____
_____

Materials:
_____
_____
_____

Knowledge & Competence:
_____
_____

Assignments / Assessments / EVC Statements:
_____
_____
_____
_____

Once They **EXPERIENCE** It

They Will ENGAGE In

Necessary Activity:
Think / Do
See / Listen

Likely Questions:
_____
_____
_____

Likely Difficulty:
_____
_____
_____

Cultural:
_____
_____
_____

Developmental:
_____
_____

Individual:
_____
_____
_____

That Which **EXCITES** Them

Standard: _____

Content: _____

Designation: _____

EVC Minimum:
_____
_____
_____
_____

EVC Maximum:
_____
_____
_____
_____

EXPOSE Them To It

Let Them EXPLORE It

Activities:
_____
_____

Strategies:
_____
_____

Materials:
_____
_____
_____

Knowledge & Competence:
_____
_____

Assignments / Assessments / EVC Statements:
_____
_____
_____
_____

Once They **EXPERIENCE** It

They Will ENGAGE In

Necessary Activity:
Think / Do
See / Listen

Likely Questions:
_____
_____
_____

Likely Difficulty:
_____
_____
_____

Cultural:
_____
_____
_____

Developmental:
_____
_____

Individual:
_____
_____
_____

That Which **EXCITES** Them

Educational Provision: Possession / Understanding / Competence / Value / Success

DESIGN IT
AM I LEADING, PROVOKING, AND SUPPORTING AN EDUCATIONAL PURSUIT?

Standard: _____

Content: _____

Designation: _____

| EVC Minimum:
 _____
 _____
 _____
 EVC Maximum:
 _____
 _____
 _____
 EXPOSE Them To It | **Let Them EXPLORE It**
 Activities:
 _____
 _____
 Strategies:
 _____
 _____
 Materials:
 _____
 _____ | Knowledge & Competence:
 _____
 _____
 Assignments / Assessments / EVC Statements:
 _____
 _____
 Once They EXPERIENCE It | **They Will ENGAGE In**
 Necessary Activity:
 Think / Do
 See / Listen
 Likely Questions:
 _____
 _____
 Likely Difficulty:
 _____
 _____ | Cultural:
 _____
 _____
 Developmental:
 _____
 _____
 Individual:
 _____
 _____
 That Which EXCITES Them |

Standard: _____

Content: _____

Designation: _____

| EVC Minimum:
 _____
 _____
 _____
 EVC Maximum:
 _____
 _____
 _____
 EXPOSE Them To It | **Let Them EXPLORE It**
 Activities:
 _____
 _____
 Strategies:
 _____
 _____
 Materials:
 _____
 _____ | Knowledge & Competence:
 _____
 _____
 Assignments / Assessments / EVC Statements:
 _____
 _____
 Once They EXPERIENCE It | **They Will ENGAGE In**
 Necessary Activity:
 Think / Do
 See / Listen
 Likely Questions:
 _____
 _____
 Likely Difficulty:
 _____
 _____ | Cultural:
 _____
 _____
 Developmental:
 _____
 _____
 Individual:
 _____
 _____
 That Which EXCITES Them |

Instructional Level: Caregiver / Teacher / Educator / Profound Mentor / Intense Trainer

DESIGN IT
DID I FACILITATE THE EDUCATIONAL PROCESS AND FULFILL THE MISSION OF EDUCATION?

Unit: _____

Week Of: _____

Standard: _____

Content: _____

Designation: _____

EVC Minimum:
_____
_____
_____
_____

EVC Maximum:
_____
_____
_____
_____

EXPOSE Them To It

Let Them EXPLORE It

Activities:
_____
_____

Strategies:
_____
_____

Materials:
_____
_____
_____

Knowledge & Competence:
_____
_____
_____

Assignments / Assessments / EVC Statements:
_____
_____
_____

Once They **EXPERIENCE** It

They Will ENGAGE In

Necessary Activity:
Think / Do
See / Listen

Likely Questions:
_____
_____
_____

Likely Difficulty:
_____
_____
_____

Cultural:
_____
_____

Developmental:
_____
_____

Individual:
_____
_____

That Which **EXCITES** Them

Standard: _____

Content: _____

Designation: _____

EVC Minimum:
_____
_____
_____
_____

EVC Maximum:
_____
_____
_____
_____

EXPOSE Them To It

Let Them EXPLORE It

Activities:
_____
_____

Strategies:
_____
_____

Materials:
_____
_____
_____

Knowledge & Competence:
_____
_____
_____

Assignments / Assessments / EVC Statements:
_____
_____
_____

Once They **EXPERIENCE** It

They Will ENGAGE In

Necessary Activity:
Think / Do
See / Listen

Likely Questions:
_____
_____
_____

Likely Difficulty:
_____
_____
_____

Cultural:
_____
_____

Developmental:
_____
_____

Individual:
_____
_____

That Which **EXCITES** Them

Educational Provision: Possession / Understanding / Competence / Value / Success

DESIGN IT
AM I LEADING, PROVOKING, AND SUPPORTING AN EDUCATIONAL PURSUIT?

Standard: _____

Content: _____

Designation: _____

EVC Minimum:
_____
_____
_____
_____

EVC Maximum:
_____
_____
_____
_____
_____

EXPOSE Them To It

Let Them EXPLORE It

Activities:
_____
_____

Strategies:
_____
_____

Materials:
_____
_____
_____

Knowledge & Competence:
_____
_____
_____

Assignments / Assessments / EVC Statements:
_____
_____
_____
_____

Once They **EXPERIENCE** It

They Will ENGAGE In

Necessary Activity:
Think / Do
See / Listen

Likely Questions:
_____
_____
_____

Likely Difficulty:
_____
_____
_____

Cultural:
_____
_____
_____

Developmental:
_____
_____
_____

Individual:
_____
_____
_____

That Which **EXCITES** Them

Standard: _____

Content: _____

Designation: _____

EVC Minimum:
_____
_____
_____
_____

EVC Maximum:
_____
_____
_____
_____
_____

EXPOSE Them To It

Let Them EXPLORE It

Activities:
_____
_____

Strategies:
_____
_____

Materials:
_____
_____
_____

Knowledge & Competence:
_____
_____
_____

Assignments / Assessments / EVC Statements:
_____
_____
_____
_____

Once They **EXPERIENCE** It

They Will ENGAGE In

Necessary Activity:
Think / Do
See / Listen

Likely Questions:
_____
_____
_____

Likely Difficulty:
_____
_____
_____

Cultural:
_____
_____
_____

Developmental:
_____
_____
_____

Individual:
_____
_____
_____

That Which **EXCITES** Them

Instructional Level: Caregiver / Teacher / Educator / Profound Mentor / Intense Trainer

DESIGN IT
Did I Facilitate The Educational Process And Fulfill The Mission Of Education?

Unit: _____

Week Of: _____

Standard: _____

Content: _____

Designation: _____

EVC Minimum:
_____
_____
_____

EVC Maximum:
_____
_____
_____
_____

EXPOSE Them To It

Let Them EXPLORE It

Activities:
_____
_____

Strategies:
_____
_____

Materials:
_____
_____
_____

Knowledge & Competence:
_____
_____
_____

Assignments / Assessments / EVC Statements:
_____
_____
_____
_____

Once They EXPERIENCE It

They Will ENGAGE In

Necessary Activity:
Think / Do
See / Listen

Likely Questions:
_____
_____
_____

Likely Difficulty:
_____
_____
_____

Cultural:
_____
_____

Developmental:
_____
_____

Individual:
_____
_____

That Which EXCITES Them

Standard: _____

Content: _____

Designation: _____

EVC Minimum:
_____
_____
_____

EVC Maximum:
_____
_____
_____
_____

EXPOSE Them To It

Let Them EXPLORE It

Activities:
_____
_____

Strategies:
_____
_____

Materials:
_____
_____
_____

Knowledge & Competence:
_____
_____
_____

Assignments / Assessments / EVC Statements:
_____
_____
_____
_____

Once They EXPERIENCE It

They Will ENGAGE In

Necessary Activity:
Think / Do
See / Listen

Likely Questions:
_____
_____
_____

Likely Difficulty:
_____
_____
_____

Cultural:
_____
_____

Developmental:
_____
_____

Individual:
_____
_____

That Which EXCITES Them

Educational Provision: Possession / Understanding / Competence / Value / Success

DESIGN IT
AM I LEADING, PROVOKING, AND SUPPORTING AN EDUCATIONAL PURSUIT?

Standard: _____

Content: _____

Designation: _____

EVC Minimum:
_____
_____
_____
_____

EVC Maximum:
_____
_____
_____
_____

EXPOSE Them To It

Let Them EXPLORE It

Activities:
_____
_____
_____

Strategies:
_____
_____

Materials:
_____
_____
_____

Knowledge & Competence:
_____
_____
_____

Assignments / Assessments / EVC Statements:
_____
_____
_____
_____

Once They **EXPERIENCE** It

They Will ENGAGE In

Necessary Activity:
Think / Do
See / Listen

Likely Questions:
_____
_____
_____

Likely Difficulty:
_____
_____
_____

Cultural:
_____
_____
_____

Developmental:
_____
_____

Individual:
_____
_____

That Which **EXCITES** Them

Standard: _____

Content: _____

Designation: _____

EVC Minimum:
_____
_____
_____
_____

EVC Maximum:
_____
_____
_____
_____

EXPOSE Them To It

Let Them EXPLORE It

Activities:
_____
_____
_____

Strategies:
_____
_____

Materials:
_____
_____
_____

Knowledge & Competence:
_____
_____
_____

Assignments / Assessments / EVC Statements:
_____
_____
_____
_____

Once They **EXPERIENCE** It

They Will ENGAGE In

Necessary Activity:
Think / Do
See / Listen

Likely Questions:
_____
_____
_____

Likely Difficulty:
_____
_____
_____

Cultural:
_____
_____
_____

Developmental:
_____
_____

Individual:
_____
_____

That Which **EXCITES** Them

Instructional Level: Caregiver / Teacher / Educator / Profound Mentor / Intense Trainer

DESIGN IT
Did I Facilitate The Educational Process And Fulfill The Mission Of Education?

Unit: _____

Week Of: _____

Standard: _____

Content: _____

Designation: _____

EVC Minimum:

_____

_____

_____

_____

EVC Maximum:

_____

_____

_____

EXPOSE Them To It

Let Them EXPLORE It

Activities:

_____

_____

Strategies:

_____

_____

Materials:

_____

_____

_____

Knowledge & Competence:

_____

_____

_____

Assignments / Assessments / EVC Statements:

_____

_____

_____

Once They EXPERIENCE It

They Will ENGAGE In

Necessary Activity:
Think / Do
See / Listen

Likely Questions:

_____

_____

_____

Likely Difficulty:

_____

_____

Cultural:

_____

_____

Developmental:

_____

_____

Individual:

_____

_____

That Which EXCITES Them

Standard: _____

Content: _____

Designation: _____

EVC Minimum:

_____

_____

_____

_____

EVC Maximum:

_____

_____

_____

EXPOSE Them To It

Let Them EXPLORE It

Activities:

_____

_____

Strategies:

_____

_____

Materials:

_____

_____

_____

Knowledge & Competence:

_____

_____

_____

Assignments / Assessments / EVC Statements:

_____

_____

_____

Once They EXPERIENCE It

They Will ENGAGE In

Necessary Activity:
Think / Do
See / Listen

Likely Questions:

_____

_____

_____

Likely Difficulty:

_____

_____

Cultural:

_____

_____

Developmental:

_____

_____

Individual:

_____

_____

That Which EXCITES Them

Educational Provision: Possession / Understanding / Competence / Value / Success

DESIGN IT
AM I LEADING, PROVOKING, AND SUPPORTING AN EDUCATIONAL PURSUIT?

Standard: _____

Content: _____

Designation: _____

EVC Minimum:	**Let Them EXPLORE It**		**They Will ENGAGE In**	
	Activities:	Knowledge & Competence:	**Necessary Activity:** Think / Do See / Listen	Cultural:
	Strategies:	Assignments / Assessments / EVC Statements:	**Likely Questions:**	Developmental:
EVC Maximum:	Materials:		**Likely Difficulty:**	Individual:
EXPOSE Them To It		**Once They EXPERIENCE It**		**That Which EXCITES Them**

Standard: _____

Content: _____

Designation: _____

EVC Minimum:	**Let Them EXPLORE It**		**They Will ENGAGE In**	
	Activities:	Knowledge & Competence:	**Necessary Activity:** Think / Do See / Listen	Cultural:
	Strategies:	Assignments / Assessments / EVC Statements:	**Likely Questions:**	Developmental:
EVC Maximum:	Materials:		**Likely Difficulty:**	Individual:
EXPOSE Them To It		**Once They EXPERIENCE It**		**That Which EXCITES Them**

Instructional Level: Caregiver   /   Teacher   /   Educator   /   Profound Mentor   /   Intense Trainer

DESIGN IT
DID I FACILITATE THE EDUCATIONAL PROCESS AND FULFILL THE MISSION OF EDUCATION?

Unit: _____

Week Of: _____

Standard: _____

Content: _____

Designation: _____

EVC Minimum:

_____
_____
_____

EVC Maximum:

_____
_____
_____

EXPOSE Them To It

Let Them EXPLORE It

Activities:

_____
_____

Strategies:

_____
_____

Materials:

_____
_____
_____

Knowledge & Competence:

_____
_____

Assignments / Assessments / EVC Statements:

_____
_____
_____

Once They **EXPERIENCE** It

They Will ENGAGE In

Necessary Activity:
Think / Do
See / Listen

Likely Questions:

_____
_____
_____

Likely Difficulty:

_____
_____
_____

Cultural:

_____
_____

Developmental:

_____
_____

Individual:

_____
_____
_____

That Which **EXCITES** Them

Standard: _____

Content: _____

Designation: _____

EVC Minimum:

_____
_____
_____

EVC Maximum:

_____
_____
_____

EXPOSE Them To It

Let Them EXPLORE It

Activities:

_____
_____

Strategies:

_____
_____

Materials:

_____
_____
_____

Knowledge & Competence:

_____
_____

Assignments / Assessments / EVC Statements:

_____
_____
_____

Once They **EXPERIENCE** It

They Will ENGAGE In

Necessary Activity:
Think / Do
See / Listen

Likely Questions:

_____
_____
_____

Likely Difficulty:

_____
_____
_____

Cultural:

_____
_____

Developmental:

_____
_____

Individual:

_____
_____
_____

That Which **EXCITES** Them

Educational Provision: Possession / Understanding / Competence / Value / Success

DESIGN IT
AM I LEADING, PROVOKING, AND SUPPORTING AN EDUCATIONAL PURSUIT?

Standard: _____

Content: _____

Designation: _____

EVC Minimum:
_____
_____
_____
_____

EVC Maximum:
_____
_____
_____
_____

EXPOSE Them To It

Let Them EXPLORE It

Activities:
_____
_____

Strategies:
_____
_____

Materials:
_____
_____

Knowledge & Competence:
_____
_____
_____

Assignments / Assessments / EVC Statements:
_____
_____
_____

Once They **EXPERIENCE** It

They Will ENGAGE In

Necessary Activity:
Think / Do
See / Listen

Likely Questions:
_____
_____
_____

Likely Difficulty:
_____
_____
_____

Cultural:
_____
_____

Developmental:
_____
_____

Individual:
_____
_____

That Which **EXCITES** Them

Standard: _____

Content: _____

Designation: _____

EVC Minimum:
_____
_____
_____
_____

EVC Maximum:
_____
_____
_____
_____

EXPOSE Them To It

Let Them EXPLORE It

Activities:
_____
_____

Strategies:
_____
_____

Materials:
_____
_____

Knowledge & Competence:
_____
_____
_____

Assignments / Assessments / EVC Statements:
_____
_____
_____

Once They **EXPERIENCE** It

They Will ENGAGE In

Necessary Activity:
Think / Do
See / Listen

Likely Questions:
_____
_____
_____

Likely Difficulty:
_____
_____
_____

Cultural:
_____
_____

Developmental:
_____
_____

Individual:
_____
_____

That Which **EXCITES** Them

Instructional Level: Caregiver / Teacher / Educator / Profound Mentor / Intense Trainer

DESIGN IT
DID I FACILITATE THE EDUCATIONAL PROCESS AND FULFILL THE MISSION OF EDUCATION?

Unit: _____

Week Of: _____

Standard: _____

Content: _____

Designation: _____

Let Them EXPLORE It

They Will ENGAGE In

EVC Minimum:	Activities:	Knowledge & Competence:	Necessary Activity: Think / Do See / Listen	Cultural:
_____	_____	_____		_____
_____	_____	_____	**Likely Questions:**	_____
_____	**Strategies:**	_____	_____	**Developmental:**
_____	_____	**Assignments / Assessments / EVC Statements:**	_____	_____
EVC Maximum:	_____	_____	_____	_____
_____	**Materials:**	_____	**Likely Difficulty:**	**Individual:**
_____	_____	_____	_____	_____
_____	_____	_____	_____	_____
_____	_____	_____	_____	_____

EXPOSE Them To It

Once They EXPERIENCE It

That Which EXCITES Them

Standard: _____

Content: _____

Designation: _____

Let Them EXPLORE It

They Will ENGAGE In

EVC Minimum:	Activities:	Knowledge & Competence:	Necessary Activity: Think / Do See / Listen	Cultural:
_____	_____	_____		_____
_____	_____	_____	**Likely Questions:**	_____
_____	**Strategies:**	_____	_____	**Developmental:**
_____	_____	**Assignments / Assessments / EVC Statements:**	_____	_____
EVC Maximum:	_____	_____	_____	_____
_____	**Materials:**	_____	**Likely Difficulty:**	**Individual:**
_____	_____	_____	_____	_____
_____	_____	_____	_____	_____
_____	_____	_____	_____	_____

EXPOSE Them To It

Once They EXPERIENCE It

That Which EXCITES Them

Educational Provision: Possession / Understanding / Competence / Value / Success

DESIGN IT
AM I LEADING, PROVOKING, AND SUPPORTING AN EDUCATIONAL PURSUIT?

Standard: _____

Content: _____

Designation: _____

EVC Minimum:
_____
_____
_____
_____

EVC Maximum:
_____
_____
_____

EXPOSE Them To It

Let Them EXPLORE It

Activities:
_____
_____
_____

Strategies:
_____
_____

Materials:
_____
_____
_____

Knowledge & Competence:
_____
_____
_____

Assignments / Assessments / EVC Statements:
_____
_____
_____

Once They EXPERIENCE It

They Will ENGAGE In

Necessary Activity:
Think / Do
See / Listen

Likely Questions:
_____
_____
_____

Likely Difficulty:
_____
_____
_____

Cultural:
_____
_____
_____

Developmental:
_____

Individual:
_____

That Which EXCITES Them

Standard: _____

Content: _____

Designation: _____

EVC Minimum:
_____
_____
_____
_____

EVC Maximum:
_____
_____
_____

EXPOSE Them To It

Let Them EXPLORE It

Activities:
_____
_____
_____

Strategies:
_____
_____

Materials:
_____
_____
_____

Knowledge & Competence:
_____
_____
_____

Assignments / Assessments / EVC Statements:
_____
_____
_____

Once They EXPERIENCE It

They Will ENGAGE In

Necessary Activity:
Think / Do
See / Listen

Likely Questions:
_____
_____
_____

Likely Difficulty:
_____
_____
_____

Cultural:
_____
_____
_____

Developmental:
_____

Individual:
_____

That Which EXCITES Them

Instructional Level: Caregiver / Teacher / Educator / Profound Mentor / Intense Trainer

DESIGN IT
DID I FACILITATE THE EDUCATIONAL PROCESS AND FULFILL THE MISSION OF EDUCATION?

Unit: _____

Week Of: _____

Standard: _____

Content: _____

Designation: _____

EVC Minimum:
_____
_____
_____
_____

EVC Maximum:
_____
_____
_____
_____

EXPOSE Them To It

Let Them EXPLORE It

Activities:
_____
_____

Strategies:
_____
_____

Materials:
_____
_____

Knowledge & Competence:
_____
_____
_____

Assignments / Assessments / EVC Statements:
_____
_____
_____

Once They EXPERIENCE It

They Will ENGAGE In

Necessary Activity:
Think / Do
See / Listen

Likely Questions:
_____
_____
_____

Likely Difficulty:
_____
_____
_____

Cultural:
_____
_____
_____

Developmental:
_____
_____

Individual:
_____
_____

That Which EXCITES Them

Standard: _____

Content: _____

Designation: _____

EVC Minimum:
_____
_____
_____
_____

EVC Maximum:
_____
_____
_____
_____

EXPOSE Them To It

Let Them EXPLORE It

Activities:
_____
_____

Strategies:
_____
_____

Materials:
_____
_____

Knowledge & Competence:
_____
_____
_____

Assignments / Assessments / EVC Statements:
_____
_____
_____

Once They EXPERIENCE It

They Will ENGAGE In

Necessary Activity:
Think / Do
See / Listen

Likely Questions:
_____
_____
_____

Likely Difficulty:
_____
_____
_____

Cultural:
_____
_____
_____

Developmental:
_____
_____

Individual:
_____
_____

That Which EXCITES Them

Educational Provision: Possession / Understanding / Competence / Value / Success

DESIGN IT
AM I LEADING, PROVOKING, AND SUPPORTING AN EDUCATIONAL PURSUIT?

Standard: _____

Content: _____

Designation: _____

EVC Minimum:	**Let Them EXPLORE It**		**They Will ENGAGE In**	
_____	Activities:	Knowledge & Competence:	**Necessary Activity:** Think / Do See / Listen	Cultural: _____
_____	_____	_____	**Likely Questions:**	_____
_____	Strategies:	_____	_____	Developmental: _____
EVC Maximum:	_____	Assignments / Assessments / EVC Statements:	_____	_____
_____	Materials:	_____	**Likely Difficulty:**	Individual: _____
_____	_____	_____	_____	_____
EXPOSE Them To It		**Once They EXPERIENCE** It		**That Which EXCITES** Them

Standard: _____

Content: _____

Designation: _____

EVC Minimum:	**Let Them EXPLORE It**		**They Will ENGAGE In**	
_____	Activities:	Knowledge & Competence:	**Necessary Activity:** Think / Do See / Listen	Cultural: _____
_____	_____	_____	**Likely Questions:**	_____
_____	Strategies:	_____	_____	Developmental: _____
EVC Maximum:	_____	Assignments / Assessments / EVC Statements:	_____	_____
_____	Materials:	_____	**Likely Difficulty:**	Individual: _____
_____	_____	_____	_____	_____
EXPOSE Them To It		**Once They EXPERIENCE** It		**That Which EXCITES** Them

Instructional Level: Caregiver   /   Teacher   /   Educator   /   Profound Mentor   /   Intense Trainer

DESIGN IT

Did I Facilitate The Educational Process And Fulfill The Mission Of Education?

Unit: _____

Week Of: _____

Standard: _____

Content: _____

Designation: _____

EVC Minimum:	Let Them **EXPLORE** It	Knowledge & Competence:	They Will **ENGAGE** In	Cultural:
_____ _____ _____ _____	Activities: _____ _____	_____ _____	Necessary Activity: Think / Do See / Listen	_____ _____
EVC Maximum:	Strategies: _____	Assignments / Assessments / EVC Statements:	Likely Questions: _____ _____	Developmental: _____
_____ _____ _____ _____	Materials: _____ _____	_____ _____ _____	Likely Difficulty: _____ _____	Individual: _____ _____
EXPOSE Them To It		Once They **EXPERIENCE** It		That Which **EXCITES** Them

Standard: _____

Content: _____

Designation: _____

EVC Minimum:	Let Them **EXPLORE** It	Knowledge & Competence:	They Will **ENGAGE** In	Cultural:
_____ _____ _____ _____	Activities: _____ _____	_____ _____	Necessary Activity: Think / Do See / Listen	_____ _____
EVC Maximum:	Strategies: _____	Assignments / Assessments / EVC Statements:	Likely Questions: _____ _____	Developmental: _____
_____ _____ _____ _____	Materials: _____ _____	_____ _____ _____	Likely Difficulty: _____ _____	Individual: _____ _____
EXPOSE Them To It		Once They **EXPERIENCE** It		That Which **EXCITES** Them

Educational Provision: Possession / Understanding / Competence / Value / Success

DESIGN IT
AM I LEADING, PROVOKING, AND SUPPORTING AN EDUCATIONAL PURSUIT?

Standard: _____

Content: _____

Designation: _____

| EVC Minimum: _____ _____ _____ _____ EVC Maximum: _____ _____ _____ _____ **EXPOSE** Them To It | **Let Them EXPLORE It** Activities: _____ _____ Strategies: _____ Materials: _____ | Knowledge & Competence: _____ _____ Assignments / Assessments / EVC Statements: _____ _____ _____ **Once They EXPERIENCE It** | **They Will ENGAGE In** **Necessary Activity:** Think / Do See / Listen **Likely Questions:** _____ _____ **Likely Difficulty:** _____ _____ | Cultural: _____ _____ Developmental: _____ _____ Individual: _____ _____ **That Which EXCITES Them** |

Standard: _____

Content: _____

Designation: _____

| EVC Minimum: _____ _____ _____ _____ EVC Maximum: _____ _____ _____ _____ **EXPOSE** Them To It | **Let Them EXPLORE It** Activities: _____ _____ Strategies: _____ Materials: _____ | Knowledge & Competence: _____ _____ Assignments / Assessments / EVC Statements: _____ _____ _____ **Once They EXPERIENCE It** | **They Will ENGAGE In** **Necessary Activity:** Think / Do See / Listen **Likely Questions:** _____ _____ **Likely Difficulty:** _____ _____ | Cultural: _____ _____ Developmental: _____ _____ Individual: _____ _____ **That Which EXCITES Them** |

Instructional Level: Caregiver / Teacher / Educator / Profound Mentor / Intense Trainer

DESIGN IT

Did I Facilitate The Educational Process And Fulfill The Mission Of Education?

Unit: _____

Week Of: _____

Standard: _____

Content: _____

Designation: _____

EVC Minimum:

_____
_____
_____

EVC Maximum:

_____
_____
_____

EXPOSE Them To It

Let Them EXPLORE It

Activities:

_____
_____

Strategies:

_____
_____

Materials:

_____
_____

Knowledge & Competence:

_____
_____

Assignments / Assessments / EVC Statements:

_____
_____
_____
_____

Once They EXPERIENCE It

They Will ENGAGE In

Necessary Activity:
Think / Do
See / Listen

Likely Questions:

_____
_____
_____

Likely Difficulty:

_____
_____
_____

Cultural:

_____
_____

Developmental:

_____
_____

Individual:

_____
_____

That Which EXCITES Them

Standard: _____

Content: _____

Designation: _____

EVC Minimum:

_____
_____
_____

EVC Maximum:

_____
_____
_____

EXPOSE Them To It

Let Them EXPLORE It

Activities:

_____
_____

Strategies:

_____
_____

Materials:

_____
_____

Knowledge & Competence:

_____
_____

Assignments / Assessments / EVC Statements:

_____
_____
_____
_____

Once They EXPERIENCE It

They Will ENGAGE In

Necessary Activity:
Think / Do
See / Listen

Likely Questions:

_____
_____
_____

Likely Difficulty:

_____
_____
_____

Cultural:

_____
_____

Developmental:

_____
_____

Individual:

_____
_____

That Which EXCITES Them

Educational Provision: Possession / Understanding / Competence / Value / Success

DESIGN IT
AM I LEADING, PROVOKING, AND SUPPORTING AN EDUCATIONAL PURSUIT?

Standard: _____

Content: _____

Designation: _____

EVC Minimum:
_____
_____
_____

EVC Maximum:
_____
_____
_____

EXPOSE Them To It

Let Them EXPLORE It

Activities:
_____
_____

Strategies:
_____
_____

Materials:
_____
_____

Knowledge & Competence:
_____
_____

Assignments / Assessments / EVC Statements:
_____
_____
_____

Once They **EXPERIENCE** It

They Will ENGAGE In

Necessary Activity:
Think / Do
See / Listen

Likely Questions:
_____
_____

Likely Difficulty:
_____
_____

Cultural:
_____
_____

Developmental:
_____
_____

Individual:
_____
_____

That Which **EXCITES** Them

Standard: _____

Content: _____

Designation: _____

EVC Minimum:
_____
_____
_____

EVC Maximum:
_____
_____
_____

EXPOSE Them To It

Let Them EXPLORE It

Activities:
_____
_____

Strategies:
_____
_____

Materials:
_____
_____

Knowledge & Competence:
_____
_____

Assignments / Assessments / EVC Statements:
_____
_____
_____

Once They **EXPERIENCE** It

They Will ENGAGE In

Necessary Activity:
Think / Do
See / Listen

Likely Questions:
_____
_____

Likely Difficulty:
_____
_____

Cultural:
_____
_____

Developmental:
_____
_____

Individual:
_____
_____

That Which **EXCITES** Them

Instructional Level: Caregiver / Teacher / Educator / Profound Mentor / Intense Trainer

DESIGN IT
Did I Facilitate The Educational Process And Fulfill The Mission Of Education?

Unit: _____

Week Of: _____

Standard: _____

Content: _____

Designation: _____

EVC Minimum:

_____

_____

_____

EVC Maximum:

_____

_____

_____

EXPOSE Them To It

Let Them EXPLORE It

Activities:

_____

_____

Strategies:

_____

_____

Materials:

_____

_____

Knowledge & Competence:

_____

_____

Assignments / Assessments / EVC Statements:

_____

_____

_____

Once They **EXPERIENCE** It

They Will ENGAGE In

Necessary Activity:
Think / Do
See / Listen

Likely Questions:

_____

_____

Likely Difficulty:

_____

_____

Cultural:

_____

_____

Developmental:

_____

_____

Individual:

_____

_____

That Which **EXCITES** Them

Standard: _____

Content: _____

Designation: _____

EVC Minimum:

_____

_____

_____

EVC Maximum:

_____

_____

_____

EXPOSE Them To It

Let Them EXPLORE It

Activities:

_____

_____

Strategies:

_____

_____

Materials:

_____

_____

Knowledge & Competence:

_____

_____

Assignments / Assessments / EVC Statements:

_____

_____

_____

Once They **EXPERIENCE** It

They Will ENGAGE In

Necessary Activity:
Think / Do
See / Listen

Likely Questions:

_____

_____

Likely Difficulty:

_____

_____

Cultural:

_____

_____

Developmental:

_____

_____

Individual:

_____

_____

That Which **EXCITES** Them

Educational Provision: Possession   /   Understanding   /   Competence   /   Value   /   Success

DESIGN IT
AM I LEADING, PROVOKING, AND SUPPORTING AN EDUCATIONAL PURSUIT?

Standard: _____

Content: _____

Designation: _____

EVC Minimum:
_____
_____
_____
_____

EVC Maximum:
_____
_____
_____
_____

EXPOSE Them To It

Let Them EXPLORE It

Activities:
_____
_____

Strategies:
_____
_____

Materials:
_____
_____

Knowledge & Competence:
_____
_____

Assignments / Assessments / EVC Statements:
_____
_____
_____

Once They **EXPERIENCE** It

They Will ENGAGE In

Necessary Activity:
Think / Do
See / Listen

Likely Questions:
_____
_____

Likely Difficulty:
_____
_____

Cultural:
_____
_____

Developmental:
_____
_____

Individual:
_____
_____

That Which **EXCITES** Them

Standard: _____

Content: _____

Designation: _____

EVC Minimum:
_____
_____
_____
_____

EVC Maximum:
_____
_____
_____
_____

EXPOSE Them To It

Let Them EXPLORE It

Activities:
_____
_____

Strategies:
_____
_____

Materials:
_____
_____

Knowledge & Competence:
_____
_____

Assignments / Assessments / EVC Statements:
_____
_____
_____

Once They **EXPERIENCE** It

They Will ENGAGE In

Necessary Activity:
Think / Do
See / Listen

Likely Questions:
_____
_____

Likely Difficulty:
_____
_____

Cultural:
_____
_____

Developmental:
_____
_____

Individual:
_____
_____

That Which **EXCITES** Them

Instructional Level: Caregiver / Teacher / Educator / Profound Mentor / Intense Trainer

DESIGN IT

DID I FACILITATE THE EDUCATIONAL PROCESS AND FULFILL THE MISSION OF EDUCATION?

Unit: _____

Week Of: _____

Standard: _____

Content: _____

Designation: _____

EVC Minimum:

_____
_____
_____
_____

EVC Maximum:

_____
_____
_____
_____

EXPOSE Them To It

Let Them EXPLORE It

Activities:

_____
_____

Strategies:

_____
_____

Materials:

_____
_____
_____

Knowledge & Competence:

_____
_____
_____

Assignments / Assessments / EVC Statements:

_____
_____
_____
_____

Once They EXPERIENCE It

They Will ENGAGE In

Necessary Activity:
Think / Do
See / Listen

Likely Questions:

_____
_____
_____

Likely Difficulty:

_____
_____
_____

Cultural:

_____
_____

Developmental:

_____
_____

Individual:

_____
_____
_____

That Which EXCITES Them

Standard: _____

Content: _____

Designation: _____

EVC Minimum:

_____
_____
_____
_____

EVC Maximum:

_____
_____
_____
_____

EXPOSE Them To It

Let Them EXPLORE It

Activities:

_____
_____

Strategies:

_____
_____

Materials:

_____
_____
_____

Knowledge & Competence:

_____
_____
_____

Assignments / Assessments / EVC Statements:

_____
_____
_____
_____

Once They EXPERIENCE It

They Will ENGAGE In

Necessary Activity:
Think / Do
See / Listen

Likely Questions:

_____
_____
_____

Likely Difficulty:

_____
_____
_____

Cultural:

_____
_____

Developmental:

_____
_____

Individual:

_____
_____
_____

That Which EXCITES Them

Educational Provision: Possession / Understanding / Competence / Value / Success

DESIGN IT
AM I LEADING, PROVOKING, AND SUPPORTING AN EDUCATIONAL PURSUIT?

Standard: _____

Content: _____

Designation: _____

EVC Minimum:
_____
_____
_____
_____

EVC Maximum:
_____
_____
_____
_____

EXPOSE Them To It

Let Them EXPLORE It

Activities:
_____

Strategies:
_____

Materials:
_____

Knowledge & Competence:
_____
_____

Assignments / Assessments / EVC Statements:
_____
_____

Once They EXPERIENCE It

They Will ENGAGE In

Necessary Activity:
Think / Do
See / Listen

Likely Questions:
_____
_____

Likely Difficulty:
_____
_____

Cultural:
_____

Developmental:
_____

Individual:
_____

That Which EXCITES Them

Standard: _____

Content: _____

Designation: _____

EVC Minimum:
_____
_____
_____
_____

EVC Maximum:
_____
_____
_____
_____

EXPOSE Them To It

Let Them EXPLORE It

Activities:
_____

Strategies:
_____

Materials:
_____

Knowledge & Competence:
_____
_____

Assignments / Assessments / EVC Statements:
_____
_____

Once They EXPERIENCE It

They Will ENGAGE In

Necessary Activity:
Think / Do
See / Listen

Likely Questions:
_____
_____

Likely Difficulty:
_____
_____

Cultural:
_____

Developmental:
_____

Individual:
_____

That Which EXCITES Them

Instructional Level: Caregiver   /   Teacher   /   Educator   /   Profound Mentor   /   Intense Trainer

DESIGN IT
Did I Facilitate The Educational Process And Fulfill The Mission Of Education?

Unit: _____

Week Of: _____

Standard: _____

Content: _____

Designation: _____

EXPOSE Them To It

EVC Minimum:
_____
_____
_____
_____

EVC Maximum:
_____
_____
_____
_____

Let Them **EXPLORE** It

Activities:
_____
_____
_____

Strategies:
_____
_____

Materials:
_____
_____
_____

Once They **EXPERIENCE** It

Knowledge & Competence:
_____
_____
_____

Assignments / Assessments / EVC Statements:
_____
_____
_____
_____

They Will **ENGAGE** In

Necessary Activity:
Think / Do
See / Listen

Likely Questions:
_____
_____
_____

Likely Difficulty:
_____
_____
_____

That Which **EXCITES** Them

Cultural:
_____
_____
_____

Developmental:
_____
_____

Individual:
_____
_____
_____

Standard: _____

Content: _____

Designation: _____

EXPOSE Them To It

EVC Minimum:
_____
_____
_____
_____

EVC Maximum:
_____
_____
_____
_____

Let Them **EXPLORE** It

Activities:
_____
_____
_____

Strategies:
_____
_____

Materials:
_____
_____
_____

Once They **EXPERIENCE** It

Knowledge & Competence:
_____
_____
_____

Assignments / Assessments / EVC Statements:
_____
_____
_____
_____

They Will **ENGAGE** In

Necessary Activity:
Think / Do
See / Listen

Likely Questions:
_____
_____
_____

Likely Difficulty:
_____
_____
_____

That Which **EXCITES** Them

Cultural:
_____
_____
_____

Developmental:
_____
_____

Individual:
_____
_____
_____

Educational Provision: Possession / Understanding / Competence / Value / Success

DESIGN IT
AM I LEADING, PROVOKING, AND SUPPORTING AN EDUCATIONAL PURSUIT?

Standard: _____

Content: _____

Designation: _____

EVC Minimum:
_____
_____
_____
_____

EVC Maximum:
_____
_____
_____
_____

EXPOSE Them To It

Let Them EXPLORE It

Activities:
_____
_____

Strategies:
_____
_____

Materials:
_____
_____

Knowledge & Competence:
_____
_____
_____

Assignments / Assessments / EVC Statements:
_____
_____
_____

Once They **EXPERIENCE** It

They Will ENGAGE In

Necessary Activity:
Think / Do
See / Listen

Likely Questions:
_____
_____
_____

Likely Difficulty:
_____
_____
_____

Cultural:
_____
_____

Developmental:
_____
_____

Individual:
_____
_____

That Which **EXCITES** Them

Standard: _____

Content: _____

Designation: _____

EVC Minimum:
_____
_____
_____
_____

EVC Maximum:
_____
_____
_____
_____

EXPOSE Them To It

Let Them EXPLORE It

Activities:
_____
_____

Strategies:
_____
_____

Materials:
_____
_____

Knowledge & Competence:
_____
_____
_____

Assignments / Assessments / EVC Statements:
_____
_____
_____

Once They **EXPERIENCE** It

They Will ENGAGE In

Necessary Activity:
Think / Do
See / Listen

Likely Questions:
_____
_____
_____

Likely Difficulty:
_____
_____
_____

Cultural:
_____
_____

Developmental:
_____
_____

Individual:
_____
_____

That Which **EXCITES** Them

Instructional Level: Caregiver   /   Teacher   /   Educator   /   Profound Mentor   /   Intense Trainer

DESIGN IT
Did I Facilitate The Educational Process And Fulfill The Mission Of Education?

Unit: _____

Week Of: _____

Standard: _____

Content: _____

Designation: _____

| EVC Minimum: ___ ___ ___ ___ EVC Maximum: ___ ___ ___ ___ **EXPOSE** Them To It | **Let Them EXPLORE It** Activities: ___ ___ Strategies: ___ ___ Materials: ___ ___ | Knowledge & Competence: ___ ___ Assignments / Assessments / EVC Statements: ___ ___ ___ **Once They EXPERIENCE It** | **They Will ENGAGE In** **Necessary Activity:** Think / Do See / Listen **Likely Questions:** ___ ___ **Likely Difficulty:** ___ ___ | Cultural: ___ ___ Developmental: ___ ___ Individual: ___ ___ **That Which EXCITES Them** |

Standard: _____

Content: _____

Designation: _____

| EVC Minimum: ___ ___ ___ ___ EVC Maximum: ___ ___ ___ ___ **EXPOSE** Them To It | **Let Them EXPLORE It** Activities: ___ ___ Strategies: ___ ___ Materials: ___ ___ | Knowledge & Competence: ___ ___ Assignments / Assessments / EVC Statements: ___ ___ ___ **Once They EXPERIENCE It** | **They Will ENGAGE In** **Necessary Activity:** Think / Do See / Listen **Likely Questions:** ___ ___ **Likely Difficulty:** ___ ___ | Cultural: ___ ___ Developmental: ___ ___ Individual: ___ ___ **That Which EXCITES Them** |

Educational Provision: Possession / Understanding / Competence / Value / Success

PROGRESS REPORT

1) When I reflect on what I **EXPOSED** students to this semester, I see that:
I was successful…_____
_____
_____

I really struggled…_____
_____
_____

Moving forward…_____
_____
_____

I may need my allies…_____
_____
_____

2) When I reflect on what and how I let students **EXPLORE** this semester, I see that that:
I was successful…_____
_____
_____

I really struggled…_____
_____
_____

Moving forward…_____
_____
_____

I may need my allies…_____
_____
_____

3) When I reflect on the **EXPERIENCE** I provided students with this semester, I see that:
I was successful…_____
_____
_____

I really struggled…_____
_____
_____

Moving forward…_____
_____
_____

I may need my allies…_____
_____
_____

PROGRESS REPORT

4) When I reflect on how I required/allowed students to **ENGAGE** this semester, I see that:

I was successful…_____
_____
_____
_____

I really struggled…_____
_____
_____
_____

Moving forward…_____
_____
_____
_____

I may need my allies…_____
_____
_____
_____

5) When I reflect on what I did to **EXCITE** students this semester, I see that:

I was successful…_____
_____
_____
_____

I really struggled…_____
_____
_____
_____

Moving forward…_____
_____
_____
_____

I may need my allies…_____
_____
_____
_____

6) When I reflect on my **EDUCATIONAL PROVISION** and **INSTRUCTIONAL LEVEL**, I see that:

I was successful…_____
_____
_____
_____

I really struggled…_____
_____
_____
_____

Moving forward…_____
_____
_____
_____

I may need my allies…_____
_____
_____
_____

COURSE

SCHOOL YEAR
20 __ / __ 20

UNIT SCHEDULE

UNIT TITLE	PROJECTED TIMELINE	TIME SPENT

DESIGN IT
AM I LEADING, PROVOKING, AND SUPPORTING AN EDUCATIONAL PURSUIT?

Standard: _____

Content: _____

Designation: _____

EVC Minimum:
_____
_____
_____

EVC Maximum:
_____
_____
_____

EXPOSE Them To It

Let Them EXPLORE It

Activities:
_____
_____

Strategies:
_____
_____

Materials:
_____
_____

Knowledge & Competence:
_____
_____

Assignments / Assessments / EVC Statements:
_____
_____
_____

Once They **EXPERIENCE** It

They Will ENGAGE In

Necessary Activity:
Think / Do
See / Listen

Likely Questions:
_____
_____

Likely Difficulty:
_____
_____
_____

Cultural:
_____
_____

Developmental:
_____
_____

Individual:
_____
_____

That Which **EXCITES** Them

Standard: _____

Content: _____

Designation: _____

EVC Minimum:
_____
_____
_____

EVC Maximum:
_____
_____
_____

EXPOSE Them To It

Let Them EXPLORE It

Activities:
_____
_____

Strategies:
_____
_____

Materials:
_____
_____

Knowledge & Competence:
_____
_____

Assignments / Assessments / EVC Statements:
_____
_____
_____

Once They **EXPERIENCE** It

They Will ENGAGE In

Necessary Activity:
Think / Do
See / Listen

Likely Questions:
_____
_____

Likely Difficulty:
_____
_____
_____

Cultural:
_____
_____

Developmental:
_____
_____

Individual:
_____
_____

That Which **EXCITES** Them

Instructional Level: Caregiver / Teacher / Educator / Profound Mentor / Intense Trainer

DESIGN IT
Did I Facilitate The Educational Process And Fulfill The Mission Of Education?

Unit: _____

Week Of: _____

Standard: _____

Content: _____

Designation: _____

EVC Minimum:
_____
_____
_____
_____

EVC Maximum:
_____
_____
_____
_____

EXPOSE Them To It

Let Them EXPLORE It

Activities:
_____
_____

Strategies:
_____
_____

Materials:
_____
_____
_____

Knowledge & Competence:
_____
_____
_____

Assignments / Assessments / EVC Statements:
_____
_____
_____
_____

Once They EXPERIENCE It

They Will ENGAGE In

Necessary Activity:
Think / Do
See / Listen

Likely Questions:
_____
_____
_____

Likely Difficulty:
_____
_____
_____

Cultural:
_____
_____

Developmental:
_____
_____

Individual:
_____
_____

That Which EXCITES Them

Standard: _____

Content: _____

Designation: _____

EVC Minimum:
_____
_____
_____
_____

EVC Maximum:
_____
_____
_____
_____

EXPOSE Them To It

Let Them EXPLORE It

Activities:
_____
_____

Strategies:
_____
_____

Materials:
_____
_____
_____

Knowledge & Competence:
_____
_____
_____

Assignments / Assessments / EVC Statements:
_____
_____
_____
_____

Once They EXPERIENCE It

They Will ENGAGE In

Necessary Activity:
Think / Do
See / Listen

Likely Questions:
_____
_____
_____

Likely Difficulty:
_____
_____
_____

Cultural:
_____
_____

Developmental:
_____
_____

Individual:
_____
_____

That Which EXCITES Them

Educational Provision: Possession / Understanding / Competence / Value / Success

DESIGN IT
AM I LEADING, PROVOKING, AND SUPPORTING AN EDUCATIONAL PURSUIT?

Standard: _____

Content: _____

Designation: _____

EVC Minimum:	**Let Them EXPLORE** It		**They Will ENGAGE** In	
	Activities:	Knowledge & Competence:	Necessary Activity: Think / Do See / Listen	Cultural:
EVC Maximum:	Strategies:	Assignments / Assessments / EVC Statements:	Likely Questions:	Developmental:
	Materials:		Likely Difficulty:	Individual:
EXPOSE Them To It		Once They **EXPERIENCE** It		That Which **EXCITES** Them

Standard: _____

Content: _____

Designation: _____

EVC Minimum:	**Let Them EXPLORE** It		**They Will ENGAGE** In	
	Activities:	Knowledge & Competence:	Necessary Activity: Think / Do See / Listen	Cultural:
EVC Maximum:	Strategies:	Assignments / Assessments / EVC Statements:	Likely Questions:	Developmental:
	Materials:		Likely Difficulty:	Individual:
EXPOSE Them To It		Once They **EXPERIENCE** It		That Which **EXCITES** Them

Instructional Level: Caregiver / Teacher / Educator / Profound Mentor / Intense Trainer

DESIGN IT
DID I FACILITATE THE EDUCATIONAL PROCESS AND
FULFILL THE MISSION OF EDUCATION?

Unit: _____

Week Of: _____

Standard: _____

Content: _____

Designation: _____

EVC Minimum:
_____
_____
_____
_____

EVC Maximum:
_____
_____
_____
_____

EXPOSE Them To It

Let Them EXPLORE It

Activities:
_____
_____

Strategies:
_____
_____

Materials:
_____
_____

Knowledge & Competence:
_____
_____
_____

Assignments / Assessments / EVC Statements:
_____
_____
_____

Once They EXPERIENCE It

They Will ENGAGE In

Necessary Activity:
Think / Do
See / Listen

Likely Questions:
_____
_____
_____

Likely Difficulty:
_____
_____
_____

Cultural:
_____
_____
_____

Developmental:
_____
_____

Individual:
_____
_____

That Which EXCITES Them

Standard: _____

Content: _____

Designation: _____

EVC Minimum:
_____
_____
_____
_____

EVC Maximum:
_____
_____
_____
_____

EXPOSE Them To It

Let Them EXPLORE It

Activities:
_____
_____

Strategies:
_____
_____

Materials:
_____
_____

Knowledge & Competence:
_____
_____
_____

Assignments / Assessments / EVC Statements:
_____
_____
_____

Once They EXPERIENCE It

They Will ENGAGE In

Necessary Activity:
Think / Do
See / Listen

Likely Questions:
_____
_____
_____

Likely Difficulty:
_____
_____
_____

Cultural:
_____
_____
_____

Developmental:
_____
_____

Individual:
_____
_____

That Which EXCITES Them

Educational Provision: Possession   /   Understanding   /   Competence   /   Value   /   Success

DESIGN IT
AM I LEADING, PROVOKING, AND SUPPORTING AN EDUCATIONAL PURSUIT?

Standard: _____

Content: _____

Designation: _____

EVC Minimum: _____ _____ _____ EVC Maximum: _____ _____ _____ _____ **EXPOSE** Them To It	**Let Them EXPLORE It** Activities: _____ _____ _____ Strategies: _____ _____ Materials: _____ _____	Knowledge & Competence: _____ _____ Assignments / Assessments / EVC Statements: _____ _____ _____ **Once They EXPERIENCE It**	**They Will ENGAGE In** Necessary Activity: Think / Do See / Listen Likely Questions: _____ _____ Likely Difficulty: _____ _____	Cultural: _____ _____ Developmental: _____ _____ Individual: _____ **That Which EXCITES Them**

Standard: _____

Content: _____

Designation: _____

EVC Minimum: _____ _____ _____ EVC Maximum: _____ _____ _____ _____ **EXPOSE** Them To It	**Let Them EXPLORE It** Activities: _____ _____ _____ Strategies: _____ _____ Materials: _____ _____	Knowledge & Competence: _____ _____ Assignments / Assessments / EVC Statements: _____ _____ _____ **Once They EXPERIENCE It**	**They Will ENGAGE In** Necessary Activity: Think / Do See / Listen Likely Questions: _____ _____ Likely Difficulty: _____ _____	Cultural: _____ _____ Developmental: _____ _____ Individual: _____ **That Which EXCITES Them**

Instructional Level: Caregiver   /   Teacher   /   Educator   /   Profound Mentor   /   Intense Trainer

DESIGN IT
Did I Facilitate The Educational Process And Fulfill The Mission Of Education?

Unit: _____

Week Of: _____

Standard: _____

Content: _____

Designation: _____

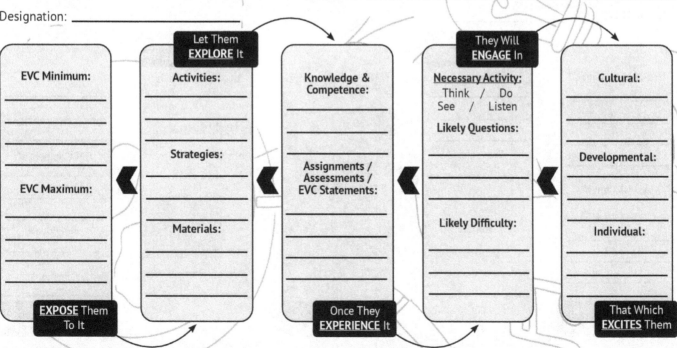

EVC Minimum:
_____
_____
_____
_____

EVC Maximum:
_____
_____
_____
_____

EXPOSE Them To It

Let Them EXPLORE It

Activities:
_____
_____

Strategies:
_____
_____

Materials:
_____
_____
_____

Knowledge & Competence:
_____
_____
_____

Assignments / Assessments / EVC Statements:
_____
_____
_____
_____

Once They **EXPERIENCE** It

They Will ENGAGE In

Necessary Activity:
Think / Do
See / Listen

Likely Questions:
_____
_____
_____

Likely Difficulty:
_____
_____
_____

Cultural:
_____
_____

Developmental:
_____
_____

Individual:
_____
_____
_____

That Which **EXCITES** Them

Standard: _____

Content: _____

Designation: _____

EVC Minimum:
_____
_____
_____
_____

EVC Maximum:
_____
_____
_____
_____

EXPOSE Them To It

Let Them EXPLORE It

Activities:
_____
_____

Strategies:
_____
_____

Materials:
_____
_____
_____

Knowledge & Competence:
_____
_____
_____

Assignments / Assessments / EVC Statements:
_____
_____
_____
_____

Once They **EXPERIENCE** It

They Will ENGAGE In

Necessary Activity:
Think / Do
See / Listen

Likely Questions:
_____
_____
_____

Likely Difficulty:
_____
_____
_____

Cultural:
_____
_____

Developmental:
_____
_____

Individual:
_____
_____
_____

That Which **EXCITES** Them

Educational Provision: Possession / Understanding / Competence / Value / Success

DESIGN IT
AM I LEADING, PROVOKING, AND SUPPORTING AN EDUCATIONAL PURSUIT?

Standard: _____

Content: _____

Designation: _____

EVC Minimum:	Let Them **EXPLORE** It		They Will **ENGAGE** In	
_____	Activities:	Knowledge & Competence:	**Necessary Activity:** Think / Do See / Listen	Cultural:
_____	_____	_____		_____
_____			**Likely Questions:**	_____
_____		_____	_____	_____
EVC Maximum:	Strategies:	Assignments / Assessments / EVC Statements:	_____	Developmental:
_____	_____		_____	_____
_____		_____	**Likely Difficulty:**	_____
_____	Materials:	_____	_____	Individual:
_____	_____	_____	_____	_____
EXPOSE Them To It		Once They **EXPERIENCE** It		That Which **EXCITES** Them

Standard: _____

Content: _____

Designation: _____

EVC Minimum:	Let Them **EXPLORE** It		They Will **ENGAGE** In	
_____	Activities:	Knowledge & Competence:	**Necessary Activity:** Think / Do See / Listen	Cultural:
_____	_____	_____		_____
_____			**Likely Questions:**	_____
_____		_____	_____	_____
EVC Maximum:	Strategies:	Assignments / Assessments / EVC Statements:	_____	Developmental:
_____	_____		_____	_____
_____		_____	**Likely Difficulty:**	_____
_____	Materials:	_____	_____	Individual:
_____	_____	_____	_____	_____
EXPOSE Them To It		Once They **EXPERIENCE** It		That Which **EXCITES** Them

Instructional Level: Caregiver   /   Teacher   /   Educator   /   Profound Mentor   /   Intense Trainer

DESIGN IT
Did I Facilitate The Educational Process And Fulfill The Mission Of Education?

Unit: _____

Week Of: _____

Standard: _____

Content: _____

Designation: _____

EVC Minimum:	Let Them **EXPLORE** It		They Will **ENGAGE** In	
	Activities:	Knowledge & Competence:	**Necessary Activity:** Think / Do See / Listen	Cultural:
	Strategies:	Assignments / Assessments / EVC Statements:	**Likely Questions:**	Developmental:
EVC Maximum:	Materials:		**Likely Difficulty:**	Individual:
EXPOSE Them To It		Once They **EXPERIENCE** It		That Which **EXCITES** Them

Standard: _____

Content: _____

Designation: _____

EVC Minimum:	Let Them **EXPLORE** It		They Will **ENGAGE** In	
	Activities:	Knowledge & Competence:	**Necessary Activity:** Think / Do See / Listen	Cultural:
	Strategies:	Assignments / Assessments / EVC Statements:	**Likely Questions:**	Developmental:
EVC Maximum:	Materials:		**Likely Difficulty:**	Individual:
EXPOSE Them To It		Once They **EXPERIENCE** It		That Which **EXCITES** Them

Educational Provision: Possession   /   Understanding   /   Competence   /   Value   /   Success

DESIGN IT
AM I LEADING, PROVOKING, AND SUPPORTING AN EDUCATIONAL PURSUIT?

Standard: _____

Content: _____

Designation: _____

EVC Minimum:	Let Them **EXPLORE** It	Knowledge & Competence:	They Will **ENGAGE** In	Cultural:
_____	Activities:	_____	**Necessary Activity:** Think / Do See / Listen	_____
_____	_____	_____	**Likely Questions:**	_____
_____	_____	_____	_____	**Developmental:**
EVC Maximum:	Strategies:	Assignments / Assessments / EVC Statements:	_____	_____
_____	_____	_____	**Likely Difficulty:**	**Individual:**
_____	Materials:	_____	_____	_____
EXPOSE Them To It		Once They **EXPERIENCE** It		That Which **EXCITES** Them

Standard: _____

Content: _____

Designation: _____

EVC Minimum:	Let Them **EXPLORE** It	Knowledge & Competence:	They Will **ENGAGE** In	Cultural:
_____	Activities:	_____	**Necessary Activity:** Think / Do See / Listen	_____
_____	_____	_____	**Likely Questions:**	_____
_____	_____	_____	_____	**Developmental:**
EVC Maximum:	Strategies:	Assignments / Assessments / EVC Statements:	_____	_____
_____	_____	_____	**Likely Difficulty:**	**Individual:**
_____	Materials:	_____	_____	_____
EXPOSE Them To It		Once They **EXPERIENCE** It		That Which **EXCITES** Them

Instructional Level: Caregiver / Teacher / Educator / Profound Mentor / Intense Trainer

DESIGN IT
Did I Facilitate The Educational Process And Fulfill The Mission Of Education?

Unit: _____

Week Of: _____

Standard: _____

Content: _____

Designation: _____

EVC Minimum:
_____
_____
_____
_____

EVC Maximum:
_____
_____
_____
_____

EXPOSE Them To It

Let Them EXPLORE It

Activities:
_____
_____

Strategies:
_____
_____

Materials:
_____
_____

Knowledge & Competence:
_____
_____

Assignments / Assessments / EVC Statements:
_____
_____
_____
_____

Once They EXPERIENCE It

They Will ENGAGE In

Necessary Activity:
Think / Do
See / Listen

Likely Questions:
_____
_____

Likely Difficulty:
_____
_____

Cultural:
_____
_____

Developmental:
_____
_____

Individual:
_____
_____

That Which EXCITES Them

Standard: _____

Content: _____

Designation: _____

EVC Minimum:
_____
_____
_____
_____

EVC Maximum:
_____
_____
_____
_____

EXPOSE Them To It

Let Them EXPLORE It

Activities:
_____
_____

Strategies:
_____
_____

Materials:
_____
_____

Knowledge & Competence:
_____
_____

Assignments / Assessments / EVC Statements:
_____
_____
_____
_____

Once They EXPERIENCE It

They Will ENGAGE In

Necessary Activity:
Think / Do
See / Listen

Likely Questions:
_____
_____

Likely Difficulty:
_____
_____

Cultural:
_____
_____

Developmental:
_____
_____

Individual:
_____
_____

That Which EXCITES Them

Educational Provision: Possession / Understanding / Competence / Value / Success

DESIGN IT
AM I LEADING, PROVOKING, AND SUPPORTING AN EDUCATIONAL PURSUIT?

Standard: _____

Content: _____

Designation: _____

| EVC Minimum: ___ ___ ___ ___ EVC Maximum: ___ ___ ___ ___ ___ **EXPOSE** Them To It | **Let Them EXPLORE It** Activities: ___ ___ Strategies: ___ ___ Materials: ___ ___ | Knowledge & Competence: ___ ___ Assignments / Assessments / EVC Statements: ___ ___ ___ ___ Once They **EXPERIENCE** It | **They Will ENGAGE In** **Necessary Activity:** Think / Do See / Listen **Likely Questions:** ___ ___ **Likely Difficulty:** ___ ___ | Cultural: ___ ___ Developmental: ___ ___ Individual: ___ ___ That Which **EXCITES** Them |

Standard: _____

Content: _____

Designation: _____

| EVC Minimum: ___ ___ ___ ___ EVC Maximum: ___ ___ ___ ___ ___ **EXPOSE** Them To It | **Let Them EXPLORE It** Activities: ___ ___ Strategies: ___ ___ Materials: ___ ___ | Knowledge & Competence: ___ ___ Assignments / Assessments / EVC Statements: ___ ___ ___ ___ Once They **EXPERIENCE** It | **They Will ENGAGE In** **Necessary Activity:** Think / Do See / Listen **Likely Questions:** ___ ___ **Likely Difficulty:** ___ ___ | Cultural: ___ ___ Developmental: ___ ___ Individual: ___ ___ That Which **EXCITES** Them |

Instructional Level: Caregiver / Teacher / Educator / Profound Mentor / Intense Trainer

DESIGN IT
DID I FACILITATE THE EDUCATIONAL PROCESS AND
FULFILL THE MISSION OF EDUCATION?

Unit: _____

Week Of: _____

Standard: _____

Content: _____

Designation: _____

EXPOSE Them To It	Let Them EXPLORE It	Once They EXPERIENCE It	They Will ENGAGE In	That Which EXCITES Them
EVC Minimum: _____ _____ _____ _____ **EVC Maximum:** _____ _____ _____ _____	**Activities:** _____ _____ **Strategies:** _____ _____ **Materials:** _____ _____	**Knowledge & Competence:** _____ _____ **Assignments / Assessments / EVC Statements:** _____ _____ _____	**Necessary Activity:** Think / Do See / Listen **Likely Questions:** _____ _____ **Likely Difficulty:** _____ _____	**Cultural:** _____ _____ **Developmental:** _____ _____ **Individual:** _____ _____

Standard: _____

Content: _____

Designation: _____

EXPOSE Them To It	Let Them EXPLORE It	Once They EXPERIENCE It	They Will ENGAGE In	That Which EXCITES Them
EVC Minimum: _____ _____ _____ _____ **EVC Maximum:** _____ _____ _____ _____	**Activities:** _____ _____ **Strategies:** _____ _____ **Materials:** _____ _____	**Knowledge & Competence:** _____ _____ **Assignments / Assessments / EVC Statements:** _____ _____ _____	**Necessary Activity:** Think / Do See / Listen **Likely Questions:** _____ _____ **Likely Difficulty:** _____ _____	**Cultural:** _____ _____ **Developmental:** _____ _____ **Individual:** _____ _____

Educational Provision: Possession / Understanding / Competence / Value / Success

DESIGN IT
AM I LEADING, PROVOKING, AND SUPPORTING AN EDUCATIONAL PURSUIT?

Standard: _____

Content: _____

Designation: _____

Let Them EXPLORE It

They Will ENGAGE In

EVC Minimum:
_____
_____
_____
_____

EVC Maximum:
_____
_____
_____
_____

EXPOSE Them To It

Activities:
_____
_____

Strategies:
_____
_____

Materials:
_____
_____

Knowledge & Competence:
_____
_____

Assignments / Assessments / EVC Statements:
_____
_____
_____

Once They EXPERIENCE It

Necessary Activity:
Think / Do
See / Listen

Likely Questions:
_____
_____
_____

Likely Difficulty:
_____
_____
_____

Cultural:
_____
_____

Developmental:
_____
_____

Individual:
_____
_____

That Which EXCITES Them

Standard: _____

Content: _____

Designation: _____

Let Them EXPLORE It

They Will ENGAGE In

EVC Minimum:
_____
_____
_____
_____

EVC Maximum:
_____
_____
_____
_____

EXPOSE Them To It

Activities:
_____
_____

Strategies:
_____
_____

Materials:
_____
_____

Knowledge & Competence:
_____
_____

Assignments / Assessments / EVC Statements:
_____
_____
_____

Once They EXPERIENCE It

Necessary Activity:
Think / Do
See / Listen

Likely Questions:
_____
_____
_____

Likely Difficulty:
_____
_____
_____

Cultural:
_____
_____

Developmental:
_____
_____

Individual:
_____
_____

That Which EXCITES Them

Instructional Level: Caregiver   /   Teacher   /   Educator   /   Profound Mentor   /   Intense Trainer

DESIGN IT
DID I FACILITATE THE EDUCATIONAL PROCESS AND FULFILL THE MISSION OF EDUCATION?

Unit: _____

Week Of: _____

Standard: _____

Content: _____

Designation: _____

EVC Minimum:
_____
_____
_____
_____

EVC Maximum:
_____
_____
_____
_____

EXPOSE Them To It

Let Them EXPLORE It

Activities:
_____
_____

Strategies:
_____
_____

Materials:
_____
_____

Knowledge & Competence:
_____
_____
_____

Assignments / Assessments / EVC Statements:
_____
_____
_____

Once They **EXPERIENCE** It

They Will ENGAGE In

Necessary Activity:
Think / Do
See / Listen

Likely Questions:
_____
_____

Likely Difficulty:
_____
_____
_____

Cultural:
_____
_____
_____

Developmental:
_____
_____

Individual:
_____
_____

That Which **EXCITES** Them

Standard: _____

Content: _____

Designation: _____

EVC Minimum:
_____
_____
_____
_____

EVC Maximum:
_____
_____
_____
_____

EXPOSE Them To It

Let Them EXPLORE It

Activities:
_____
_____

Strategies:
_____
_____

Materials:
_____
_____

Knowledge & Competence:
_____
_____
_____

Assignments / Assessments / EVC Statements:
_____
_____
_____

Once They **EXPERIENCE** It

They Will ENGAGE In

Necessary Activity:
Think / Do
See / Listen

Likely Questions:
_____
_____

Likely Difficulty:
_____
_____
_____

Cultural:
_____
_____
_____

Developmental:
_____
_____

Individual:
_____
_____

That Which **EXCITES** Them

Educational Provision:　Possession　/　Understanding　/　Competence　/　Value　/　Success

DESIGN IT
AM I LEADING, PROVOKING, AND SUPPORTING AN EDUCATIONAL PURSUIT?

Standard: _____

Content: _____

Designation: _____

Let Them EXPLORE It

They Will ENGAGE In

EVC Minimum:	Activities:	Knowledge & Competence:	Necessary Activity: Think / Do See / Listen	Cultural:
_____	_____	_____	_____	_____
_____	Strategies:	_____	Likely Questions:	_____
EVC Maximum:	_____	Assignments / Assessments / EVC Statements:	_____	Developmental:
_____	Materials:	_____	Likely Difficulty:	_____
_____	_____	_____	_____	Individual:

EXPOSE Them To It

Once They EXPERIENCE It

That Which EXCITES Them

Standard: _____

Content: _____

Designation: _____

Let Them EXPLORE It

They Will ENGAGE In

EVC Minimum:	Activities:	Knowledge & Competence:	Necessary Activity: Think / Do See / Listen	Cultural:
_____	_____	_____	_____	_____
_____	Strategies:	_____	Likely Questions:	_____
EVC Maximum:	_____	Assignments / Assessments / EVC Statements:	_____	Developmental:
_____	Materials:	_____	Likely Difficulty:	_____
_____	_____	_____	_____	Individual:

EXPOSE Them To It

Once They EXPERIENCE It

That Which EXCITES Them

Instructional Level: Caregiver   /   Teacher   /   Educator   /   Profound Mentor   /   Intense Trainer

DESIGN IT
DID I FACILITATE THE EDUCATIONAL PROCESS AND FULFILL THE MISSION OF EDUCATION?

Unit: _____

Week Of: _____

Standard: _____

Content: _____

Designation: _____

EVC Minimum:

_____

_____

_____

EVC Maximum:

_____

_____

_____

EXPOSE Them To It

Let Them EXPLORE It

Activities:

_____

Strategies:

_____

Materials:

_____

Knowledge & Competence:

_____

_____

Assignments / Assessments / EVC Statements:

_____

_____

Once They **EXPERIENCE** It

They Will ENGAGE In

Necessary Activity:
Think / Do
See / Listen

Likely Questions:

_____

_____

Likely Difficulty:

_____

_____

Cultural:

_____

_____

Developmental:

_____

Individual:

_____

That Which **EXCITES** Them

Standard: _____

Content: _____

Designation: _____

EVC Minimum:

_____

_____

_____

EVC Maximum:

_____

_____

_____

EXPOSE Them To It

Let Them EXPLORE It

Activities:

_____

Strategies:

_____

Materials:

_____

Knowledge & Competence:

_____

_____

Assignments / Assessments / EVC Statements:

_____

_____

Once They **EXPERIENCE** It

They Will ENGAGE In

Necessary Activity:
Think / Do
See / Listen

Likely Questions:

_____

_____

Likely Difficulty:

_____

_____

Cultural:

_____

_____

Developmental:

_____

Individual:

_____

That Which **EXCITES** Them

Educational Provision: Possession / Understanding / Competence / Value / Success

DESIGN IT
AM I LEADING, PROVOKING, AND SUPPORTING AN EDUCATIONAL PURSUIT?

Standard: _____

Content: _____

Designation: _____

EVC Minimum:
_____
_____
_____

EVC Maximum:
_____
_____
_____

EXPOSE Them To It

Let Them EXPLORE It

Activities:
_____

Strategies:
_____

Materials:
_____

Knowledge & Competence:
_____
_____

Assignments / Assessments / EVC Statements:
_____
_____

Once They EXPERIENCE It

They Will ENGAGE In

Necessary Activity:
Think / Do
See / Listen

Likely Questions:
_____
_____

Likely Difficulty:
_____
_____

Cultural:
_____
_____

Developmental:
_____

Individual:
_____

That Which EXCITES Them

Standard: _____

Content: _____

Designation: _____

EVC Minimum:
_____
_____
_____

EVC Maximum:
_____
_____
_____

EXPOSE Them To It

Let Them EXPLORE It

Activities:
_____

Strategies:
_____

Materials:
_____

Knowledge & Competence:
_____
_____

Assignments / Assessments / EVC Statements:
_____
_____

Once They EXPERIENCE It

They Will ENGAGE In

Necessary Activity:
Think / Do
See / Listen

Likely Questions:
_____
_____

Likely Difficulty:
_____
_____

Cultural:
_____
_____

Developmental:
_____

Individual:
_____

That Which EXCITES Them

Instructional Level: Caregiver / Teacher / Educator / Profound Mentor / Intense Trainer

DESIGN IT
Did I Facilitate The Educational Process And Fulfill The Mission Of Education?

Unit: _____

Week Of: _____

Standard: _____

Content: _____

Designation: _____

EXVC Minimum:
_____
_____
_____
_____

EVC Maximum:
_____
_____
_____
_____

EXPOSE Them To It

Let Them EXPLORE It

Activities:
_____
_____

Strategies:
_____
_____

Materials:
_____
_____

Knowledge & Competence:
_____
_____
_____

Assignments / Assessments / EVC Statements:
_____
_____
_____
_____

Once They EXPERIENCE It

They Will ENGAGE In

Necessary Activity:
Think / Do
See / Listen

Likely Questions:
_____
_____
_____

Likely Difficulty:
_____
_____
_____
_____

Cultural:
_____
_____
_____

Developmental:
_____
_____
_____

Individual:
_____
_____
_____

That Which EXCITES Them

Standard: _____

Content: _____

Designation: _____

EVC Minimum:
_____
_____
_____
_____

EVC Maximum:
_____
_____
_____
_____

EXPOSE Them To It

Let Them EXPLORE It

Activities:
_____
_____

Strategies:
_____
_____

Materials:
_____
_____

Knowledge & Competence:
_____
_____
_____

Assignments / Assessments / EVC Statements:
_____
_____
_____
_____

Once They EXPERIENCE It

They Will ENGAGE In

Necessary Activity:
Think / Do
See / Listen

Likely Questions:
_____
_____
_____

Likely Difficulty:
_____
_____
_____
_____

Cultural:
_____
_____
_____

Developmental:
_____
_____
_____

Individual:
_____
_____
_____

That Which EXCITES Them

Educational Provision: Possession / Understanding / Competence / Value / Success

DESIGN IT
AM I LEADING, PROVOKING, AND SUPPORTING AN EDUCATIONAL PURSUIT?

Standard: _____

Content: _____

Designation: _____

| EVC Minimum: _____ _____ _____ _____ EVC Maximum: _____ _____ _____ _____ **EXPOSE** Them To It | **Let Them EXPLORE It** Activities: _____ _____ Strategies: _____ _____ Materials: _____ _____ | Knowledge & Competence: _____ _____ Assignments / Assessments / EVC Statements: _____ _____ _____ **Once They EXPERIENCE It** | **They Will ENGAGE In** Necessary Activity: Think / Do See / Listen Likely Questions: _____ _____ _____ Likely Difficulty: _____ _____ _____ | Cultural: _____ _____ Developmental: _____ _____ Individual: _____ _____ **That Which EXCITES Them** |

Standard: _____

Content: _____

Designation: _____

| EVC Minimum: _____ _____ _____ EVC Maximum: _____ _____ _____ **EXPOSE** Them To It | **Let Them EXPLORE It** Activities: _____ _____ Strategies: _____ _____ Materials: _____ _____ | Knowledge & Competence: _____ _____ Assignments / Assessments / EVC Statements: _____ _____ _____ **Once They EXPERIENCE It** | **They Will ENGAGE In** Necessary Activity: Think / Do See / Listen Likely Questions: _____ _____ _____ Likely Difficulty: _____ _____ _____ | Cultural: _____ _____ Developmental: _____ _____ Individual: _____ _____ **That Which EXCITES Them** |

Instructional Level: Caregiver / Teacher / Educator / Profound Mentor / Intense Trainer

DESIGN IT
DID I FACILITATE THE EDUCATIONAL PROCESS AND FULFILL THE MISSION OF EDUCATION?

Unit: _____

Week Of: _____

Standard: _____

Content: _____

Designation: _____

EXPOSE Them To It

EVC Minimum:
_____
_____
_____

EVC Maximum:
_____
_____
_____
_____

Let Them EXPLORE It

Activities:
_____
_____

Strategies:
_____
_____

Materials:
_____
_____
_____

Once They EXPERIENCE It

Knowledge & Competence:
_____
_____

Assignments / Assessments / EVC Statements:
_____
_____
_____
_____

They Will ENGAGE In

Necessary Activity:
Think / Do
See / Listen

Likely Questions:
_____
_____

Likely Difficulty:
_____
_____
_____

That Which EXCITES Them

Cultural:
_____
_____

Developmental:
_____
_____

Individual:
_____
_____

Standard: _____

Content: _____

Designation: _____

EXPOSE Them To It

EVC Minimum:
_____
_____
_____

EVC Maximum:
_____
_____
_____
_____

Let Them EXPLORE It

Activities:
_____
_____

Strategies:
_____
_____

Materials:
_____
_____
_____

Once They EXPERIENCE It

Knowledge & Competence:
_____
_____

Assignments / Assessments / EVC Statements:
_____
_____
_____
_____

They Will ENGAGE In

Necessary Activity:
Think / Do
See / Listen

Likely Questions:
_____
_____

Likely Difficulty:
_____
_____
_____

That Which EXCITES Them

Cultural:
_____
_____

Developmental:
_____
_____

Individual:
_____
_____

Educational Provision: Possession / Understanding / Competence / Value / Success

DESIGN IT
AM I LEADING, PROVOKING, AND SUPPORTING AN EDUCATIONAL PURSUIT?

Standard: _____

Content: _____

Designation: _____

EVC Minimum:	**Let Them EXPLORE It**		**They Will ENGAGE In**	
EVC Minimum:	Activities:	Knowledge & Competence:	**Necessary Activity:** Think / Do See / Listen	Cultural:
			Likely Questions:	
EVC Maximum:	Strategies:	Assignments / Assessments / EVC Statements:		Developmental:
	Materials:		**Likely Difficulty:**	Individual:
EXPOSE Them To It		**Once They EXPERIENCE It**		**That Which EXCITES Them**

Standard: _____

Content: _____

Designation: _____

EVC Minimum:	**Let Them EXPLORE It**		**They Will ENGAGE In**	
EVC Minimum:	Activities:	Knowledge & Competence:	**Necessary Activity:** Think / Do See / Listen	Cultural:
			Likely Questions:	
EVC Maximum:	Strategies:	Assignments / Assessments / EVC Statements:		Developmental:
	Materials:		**Likely Difficulty:**	Individual:
EXPOSE Them To It		**Once They EXPERIENCE It**		**That Which EXCITES Them**

Instructional Level: Caregiver   /   Teacher   /   Educator   /   Profound Mentor   /   Intense Trainer

DESIGN IT
DID I FACILITATE THE EDUCATIONAL PROCESS AND
FULFILL THE MISSION OF EDUCATION?

Unit: _____

Week Of: _____

Standard: _____

Content: _____

Designation: _____

EXPOSE Them To It

EVC Minimum:

_____
_____
_____
_____

EVC Maximum:

_____
_____
_____
_____

Let Them EXPLORE It

Activities:

_____
_____

Strategies:

_____
_____

Materials:

_____
_____
_____

Once They EXPERIENCE It

Knowledge & Competence:

_____
_____
_____

Assignments / Assessments / EVC Statements:

_____
_____
_____
_____

They Will ENGAGE In

Necessary Activity:
Think / Do
See / Listen

Likely Questions:

_____
_____
_____

Likely Difficulty:

_____
_____
_____

That Which EXCITES Them

Cultural:

_____
_____

Developmental:

_____
_____

Individual:

_____
_____
_____

Standard: _____

Content: _____

Designation: _____

EXPOSE Them To It

EVC Minimum:

_____
_____
_____
_____

EVC Maximum:

_____
_____
_____
_____

Let Them EXPLORE It

Activities:

_____
_____

Strategies:

_____
_____

Materials:

_____
_____
_____

Once They EXPERIENCE It

Knowledge & Competence:

_____
_____
_____

Assignments / Assessments / EVC Statements:

_____
_____
_____
_____

They Will ENGAGE In

Necessary Activity:
Think / Do
See / Listen

Likely Questions:

_____
_____
_____

Likely Difficulty:

_____
_____
_____

That Which EXCITES Them

Cultural:

_____
_____

Developmental:

_____
_____

Individual:

_____
_____
_____

Educational Provision: Possession / Understanding / Competence / Value / Success

DESIGN IT
AM I LEADING, PROVOKING, AND SUPPORTING AN EDUCATIONAL PURSUIT?

Standard: _____

Content: _____

Designation: _____

EVC Minimum:
_____
_____
_____
_____

EVC Maximum:
_____
_____
_____
_____

EXPOSE Them To It

Let Them EXPLORE It

Activities:
_____
_____

Strategies:
_____
_____

Materials:
_____
_____

Knowledge & Competence:
_____
_____

Assignments / Assessments / EVC Statements:
_____
_____
_____
_____

Once They EXPERIENCE It

They Will ENGAGE In

Necessary Activity:
Think / Do
See / Listen

Likely Questions:
_____
_____

Likely Difficulty:
_____
_____

Cultural:
_____
_____

Developmental:
_____
_____

Individual:
_____
_____

That Which EXCITES Them

Standard: _____

Content: _____

Designation: _____

EVC Minimum:
_____
_____
_____
_____

EVC Maximum:
_____
_____
_____
_____

EXPOSE Them To It

Let Them EXPLORE It

Activities:
_____
_____

Strategies:
_____
_____

Materials:
_____
_____

Knowledge & Competence:
_____
_____

Assignments / Assessments / EVC Statements:
_____
_____
_____
_____

Once They EXPERIENCE It

They Will ENGAGE In

Necessary Activity:
Think / Do
See / Listen

Likely Questions:
_____
_____

Likely Difficulty:
_____
_____

Cultural:
_____
_____

Developmental:
_____
_____

Individual:
_____
_____

That Which EXCITES Them

Instructional Level: Caregiver / Teacher / Educator / Profound Mentor / Intense Trainer

DESIGN IT
Did I Facilitate The Educational Process And Fulfill The Mission Of Education?

Unit: _____

Week Of: _____

Standard: _____

Content: _____

Designation: _____

EVC Minimum:
_____
_____
_____

EVC Maximum:
_____
_____
_____

EXPOSE Them To It

Let Them EXPLORE It

Activities:
_____
_____

Strategies:
_____
_____

Materials:
_____
_____
_____

Knowledge & Competence:
_____
_____
_____

Assignments / Assessments / EVC Statements:
_____
_____
_____

Once They **EXPERIENCE** It

They Will ENGAGE In

Necessary Activity:
Think / Do
See / Listen

Likely Questions:
_____
_____
_____

Likely Difficulty:
_____
_____
_____

Cultural:
_____
_____
_____

Developmental:
_____
_____

Individual:
_____
_____

That Which **EXCITES** Them

Standard: _____

Content: _____

Designation: _____

EVC Minimum:
_____
_____
_____

EVC Maximum:
_____
_____
_____

EXPOSE Them To It

Let Them EXPLORE It

Activities:
_____
_____

Strategies:
_____
_____

Materials:
_____
_____
_____

Knowledge & Competence:
_____
_____
_____

Assignments / Assessments / EVC Statements:
_____
_____
_____

Once They **EXPERIENCE** It

They Will ENGAGE In

Necessary Activity:
Think / Do
See / Listen

Likely Questions:
_____
_____
_____

Likely Difficulty:
_____
_____
_____

Cultural:
_____
_____
_____

Developmental:
_____
_____

Individual:
_____
_____

That Which **EXCITES** Them

Educational Provision: Possession / Understanding / Competence / Value / Success

DESIGN IT
AM I LEADING, PROVOKING, AND SUPPORTING AN EDUCATIONAL PURSUIT?

Standard: _____

Content: _____

Designation: _____

EVC Minimum:
_____
_____
_____
_____

EVC Maximum:
_____
_____
_____
_____

EXPOSE Them To It

Let Them EXPLORE It

Activities:
_____
_____

Strategies:
_____
_____

Materials:
_____
_____

Knowledge & Competence:
_____
_____

Assignments / Assessments / EVC Statements:
_____
_____
_____
_____

Once They **EXPERIENCE** It

They Will ENGAGE In

Necessary Activity:
Think / Do
See / Listen

Likely Questions:
_____
_____
_____

Likely Difficulty:
_____
_____
_____

Cultural:
_____
_____

Developmental:
_____
_____

Individual:
_____
_____

That Which **EXCITES** Them

Standard: _____

Content: _____

Designation: _____

EVC Minimum:
_____
_____
_____
_____

EVC Maximum:
_____
_____
_____
_____

EXPOSE Them To It

Let Them EXPLORE It

Activities:
_____
_____

Strategies:
_____
_____

Materials:
_____
_____

Knowledge & Competence:
_____
_____

Assignments / Assessments / EVC Statements:
_____
_____
_____
_____

Once They **EXPERIENCE** It

They Will ENGAGE In

Necessary Activity:
Think / Do
See / Listen

Likely Questions:
_____
_____
_____

Likely Difficulty:
_____
_____
_____

Cultural:
_____
_____

Developmental:
_____
_____

Individual:
_____
_____

That Which **EXCITES** Them

Instructional Level: Caregiver / Teacher / Educator / Profound Mentor / Intense Trainer

DESIGN IT
Did I Facilitate The Educational Process And Fulfill The Mission Of Education?

Unit: _____

Week Of: _____

Standard: _____

Content: _____

Designation: _____

EXPOSE Them To It

EVC Minimum:
_____
_____
_____
_____

EVC Maximum:
_____
_____
_____
_____

Let Them EXPLORE It

Activities:
_____
_____

Strategies:
_____
_____

Materials:
_____
_____
_____

Once They EXPERIENCE It

Knowledge & Competence:
_____
_____
_____

Assignments / Assessments / EVC Statements:
_____
_____
_____

They Will ENGAGE In

Necessary Activity:
Think / Do
See / Listen

Likely Questions:
_____
_____
_____

Likely Difficulty:
_____
_____

That Which EXCITES Them

Cultural:
_____
_____

Developmental:
_____
_____

Individual:
_____
_____

Standard: _____

Content: _____

Designation: _____

EXPOSE Them To It

EVC Minimum:
_____
_____
_____
_____

EVC Maximum:
_____
_____
_____
_____

Let Them EXPLORE It

Activities:
_____
_____

Strategies:
_____
_____

Materials:
_____
_____
_____

Once They EXPERIENCE It

Knowledge & Competence:
_____
_____
_____

Assignments / Assessments / EVC Statements:
_____
_____
_____

They Will ENGAGE In

Necessary Activity:
Think / Do
See / Listen

Likely Questions:
_____
_____
_____

Likely Difficulty:
_____
_____

That Which EXCITES Them

Cultural:
_____
_____

Developmental:
_____
_____

Individual:
_____
_____

Educational Provision: Possession   /   Understanding   /   Competence   /   Value   /   Success

DESIGN IT
AM I LEADING, PROVOKING, AND SUPPORTING AN EDUCATIONAL PURSUIT?

Standard: _____

Content: _____

Designation: _____

EVC Minimum:	**Let Them EXPLORE It**		**They Will ENGAGE In**	
EVC Minimum: _____ _____ _____ _____ **EVC Maximum:** _____ _____ _____ _____ **EXPOSE Them To It**	**Activities:** _____ _____ **Strategies:** _____ _____ **Materials:** _____ _____ _____	**Knowledge & Competence:** _____ _____ **Assignments / Assessments / EVC Statements:** _____ _____ _____ **Once They EXPERIENCE It**	**Necessary Activity:** Think / Do See / Listen **Likely Questions:** _____ _____ **Likely Difficulty:** _____ _____ _____	**Cultural:** _____ _____ **Developmental:** _____ _____ **Individual:** _____ _____ **That Which EXCITES Them**

Standard: _____

Content: _____

Designation: _____

| **EVC Minimum:** _____ _____ _____ _____ **EVC Maximum:** _____ _____ _____ _____ **EXPOSE Them To It** | **Activities:** _____ _____ **Strategies:** _____ _____ **Materials:** _____ _____ _____ | **Knowledge & Competence:** _____ _____ **Assignments / Assessments / EVC Statements:** _____ _____ _____ **Once They EXPERIENCE It** | **Necessary Activity:** Think / Do See / Listen **Likely Questions:** _____ _____ **Likely Difficulty:** _____ _____ _____ | **Cultural:** _____ _____ **Developmental:** _____ _____ **Individual:** _____ _____ **That Which EXCITES Them** |

Instructional Level: Caregiver / Teacher / Educator / Profound Mentor / Intense Trainer

DESIGN IT
DID I FACILITATE THE EDUCATIONAL PROCESS AND FULFILL THE MISSION OF EDUCATION?

Unit: _____

Week Of: _____

Standard: _____

Content: _____

Designation: _____

EVC Minimum:

_____

_____

_____

EVC Maximum:

_____

_____

_____

EXPOSE Them To It

Let Them EXPLORE It

Activities:

_____

_____

Strategies:

_____

_____

Materials:

_____

_____

Knowledge & Competence:

_____

_____

Assignments / Assessments / EVC Statements:

_____

_____

Once They EXPERIENCE It

They Will ENGAGE In

Necessary Activity:
Think / Do
See / Listen

Likely Questions:

_____

_____

Likely Difficulty:

_____

_____

Cultural:

_____

_____

Developmental:

_____

_____

Individual:

_____

_____

That Which EXCITES Them

Standard: _____

Content: _____

Designation: _____

EVC Minimum:

_____

_____

_____

EVC Maximum:

_____

_____

_____

EXPOSE Them To It

Let Them EXPLORE It

Activities:

_____

_____

Strategies:

_____

_____

Materials:

_____

_____

Knowledge & Competence:

_____

_____

Assignments / Assessments / EVC Statements:

_____

_____

Once They EXPERIENCE It

They Will ENGAGE In

Necessary Activity:
Think / Do
See / Listen

Likely Questions:

_____

_____

Likely Difficulty:

_____

_____

Cultural:

_____

_____

Developmental:

_____

_____

Individual:

_____

_____

That Which EXCITES Them

Educational Provision: Possession / Understanding / Competence / Value / Success

DESIGN IT
AM I LEADING, PROVOKING, AND SUPPORTING AN EDUCATIONAL PURSUIT?

Standard: _____

Content: _____

Designation: _____

| **EVC Minimum:** ____ ____ ____ ____ **EVC Maximum:** ____ ____ ____ ____ **EXPOSE** Them To It | **Let Them EXPLORE** It **Activities:** ____ ____ **Strategies:** ____ ____ **Materials:** ____ | **Knowledge & Competence:** ____ ____ **Assignments / Assessments / EVC Statements:** ____ ____ ____ **Once They EXPERIENCE** It | **They Will ENGAGE** In **Necessary Activity:** Think / Do See / Listen **Likely Questions:** ____ ____ **Likely Difficulty:** ____ ____ ____ | **Cultural:** ____ ____ **Developmental:** ____ ____ **Individual:** ____ ____ **That Which EXCITES** Them |

Standard: _____

Content: _____

Designation: _____

| **EVC Minimum:** ____ ____ ____ ____ **EVC Maximum:** ____ ____ ____ ____ **EXPOSE** Them To It | **Let Them EXPLORE** It **Activities:** ____ ____ **Strategies:** ____ ____ **Materials:** ____ | **Knowledge & Competence:** ____ ____ **Assignments / Assessments / EVC Statements:** ____ ____ ____ **Once They EXPERIENCE** It | **They Will ENGAGE** In **Necessary Activity:** Think / Do See / Listen **Likely Questions:** ____ ____ **Likely Difficulty:** ____ ____ ____ | **Cultural:** ____ ____ **Developmental:** ____ ____ **Individual:** ____ ____ **That Which EXCITES** Them |

Instructional Level: Caregiver   /   Teacher   /   Educator   /   Profound Mentor   /   Intense Trainer

DESIGN IT
DID I FACILITATE THE EDUCATIONAL PROCESS AND FULFILL THE MISSION OF EDUCATION?

Unit: _____

Week Of: _____

Standard: _____

Content: _____

Designation: _____

EXPOSE Them To It

EVC Minimum:
_____
_____
_____
_____

EVC Maximum:
_____
_____
_____
_____

Let Them EXPLORE It

Activities:
_____
_____

Strategies:
_____
_____

Materials:
_____
_____

Once They EXPERIENCE It

Knowledge & Competence:
_____
_____
_____

Assignments / Assessments / EVC Statements:
_____
_____
_____

They Will ENGAGE In

Necessary Activity:
Think / Do
See / Listen

Likely Questions:
_____
_____

Likely Difficulty:
_____
_____
_____

That Which EXCITES Them

Cultural:
_____
_____

Developmental:
_____
_____

Individual:
_____
_____

Standard: _____

Content: _____

Designation: _____

EXPOSE Them To It

EVC Minimum:
_____
_____
_____

EVC Maximum:
_____
_____
_____

Let Them EXPLORE It

Activities:
_____
_____

Strategies:
_____
_____

Materials:
_____
_____

Once They EXPERIENCE It

Knowledge & Competence:
_____
_____

Assignments / Assessments / EVC Statements:
_____
_____
_____

They Will ENGAGE In

Necessary Activity:
Think / Do
See / Listen

Likely Questions:
_____
_____

Likely Difficulty:
_____
_____

That Which EXCITES Them

Cultural:
_____
_____

Developmental:
_____
_____

Individual:
_____
_____

Educational Provision: Possession   /   Understanding   /   Competence   /   Value   /   Success

DESIGN IT
AM I LEADING, PROVOKING, AND SUPPORTING AN EDUCATIONAL PURSUIT?

Standard: _____

Content: _____

Designation: _____

EVC Minimum:
_____
_____
_____

EVC Maximum:
_____
_____
_____

EXPOSE Them To It

Let Them EXPLORE It

Activities:
_____
_____

Strategies:
_____
_____

Materials:
_____
_____

Knowledge & Competence:
_____
_____

Assignments / Assessments / EVC Statements:
_____
_____
_____

Once They **EXPERIENCE** It

They Will ENGAGE In

Necessary Activity:
Think / Do
See / Listen

Likely Questions:
_____
_____

Likely Difficulty:
_____
_____

Cultural:
_____
_____

Developmental:
_____
_____

Individual:
_____
_____

That Which **EXCITES** Them

Standard: _____

Content: _____

Designation: _____

EVC Minimum:
_____
_____
_____

EVC Maximum:
_____
_____
_____

EXPOSE Them To It

Let Them EXPLORE It

Activities:
_____
_____

Strategies:
_____
_____

Materials:
_____
_____

Knowledge & Competence:
_____
_____

Assignments / Assessments / EVC Statements:
_____
_____
_____

Once They **EXPERIENCE** It

They Will ENGAGE In

Necessary Activity:
Think / Do
See / Listen

Likely Questions:
_____
_____

Likely Difficulty:
_____
_____

Cultural:
_____
_____

Developmental:
_____
_____

Individual:
_____
_____

That Which **EXCITES** Them

Instructional Level: Caregiver / Teacher / Educator / Profound Mentor / Intense Trainer

DESIGN IT

Did I Facilitate The Educational Process And Fulfill The Mission Of Education?

Unit: _____

Week Of: _____

Standard: _____

Content: _____

Designation: _____

EVC Minimum:
_____
_____
_____

EVC Maximum:
_____
_____
_____

EXPOSE Them To It

Let Them EXPLORE It

Activities:
_____
_____

Strategies:
_____
_____

Materials:
_____

Knowledge & Competence:
_____
_____
_____

Assignments / Assessments / EVC Statements:
_____
_____
_____

Once They EXPERIENCE It

They Will ENGAGE In

Necessary Activity:
Think / Do
See / Listen

Likely Questions:
_____
_____
_____

Likely Difficulty:
_____
_____

Cultural:
_____
_____
_____

Developmental:
_____
_____

Individual:
_____
_____

That Which EXCITES Them

Standard: _____

Content: _____

Designation: _____

EVC Minimum:
_____
_____
_____

EVC Maximum:
_____
_____
_____

EXPOSE Them To It

Let Them EXPLORE It

Activities:
_____
_____

Strategies:
_____
_____

Materials:
_____

Knowledge & Competence:
_____
_____
_____

Assignments / Assessments / EVC Statements:
_____
_____
_____

Once They EXPERIENCE It

They Will ENGAGE In

Necessary Activity:
Think / Do
See / Listen

Likely Questions:
_____
_____
_____

Likely Difficulty:
_____
_____

Cultural:
_____
_____
_____

Developmental:
_____
_____

Individual:
_____
_____

That Which EXCITES Them

Educational Provision: Possession / Understanding / Competence / Value / Success

DESIGN IT
AM I LEADING, PROVOKING, AND SUPPORTING AN EDUCATIONAL PURSUIT?

Standard: _____

Content: _____

Designation: _____

EVC Minimum:	Let Them **EXPLORE** It		They Will **ENGAGE** In	
EVC Minimum: ___ ___ ___ EVC Maximum: ___ ___ ___ ___ **EXPOSE** Them To It	Activities: ___ ___ Strategies: ___ ___ Materials: ___	Knowledge & Competence: ___ ___ Assignments / Assessments / EVC Statements: ___ ___ ___ Once They **EXPERIENCE** It	Necessary Activity: Think / Do See / Listen Likely Questions: ___ ___ Likely Difficulty: ___ ___	Cultural: ___ ___ Developmental: ___ ___ Individual: ___ ___ That Which **EXCITES** Them

Standard: _____

Content: _____

Designation: _____

EVC Minimum:	Let Them **EXPLORE** It		They Will **ENGAGE** In	
EVC Minimum: ___ ___ ___ EVC Maximum: ___ ___ ___ ___ **EXPOSE** Them To It	Activities: ___ ___ Strategies: ___ ___ Materials: ___	Knowledge & Competence: ___ ___ Assignments / Assessments / EVC Statements: ___ ___ ___ Once They **EXPERIENCE** It	Necessary Activity: Think / Do See / Listen Likely Questions: ___ ___ Likely Difficulty: ___ ___	Cultural: ___ ___ Developmental: ___ ___ Individual: ___ ___ That Which **EXCITES** Them

Instructional Level: Caregiver / Teacher / Educator / Profound Mentor / Intense Trainer

DESIGN IT
Did I Facilitate The Educational Process And Fulfill The Mission Of Education?

Unit: _____

Week Of: _____

Standard: _____

Content: _____

Designation: _____

EVC Minimum:	**Let Them EXPLORE It**	Knowledge & Competence:	**They Will ENGAGE In**	Cultural:
_____ _____ _____ _____	Activities: _____ _____ _____	_____ _____ _____	**Necessary Activity:** Think / Do See / Listen	_____ _____
EVC Maximum:	Strategies: _____ _____	Assignments / Assessments / EVC Statements:	**Likely Questions:** _____ _____ _____	Developmental: _____ _____
_____ _____ _____ _____ _____	Materials: _____ _____ _____	_____ _____ _____ _____	**Likely Difficulty:** _____ _____ _____	Individual: _____ _____
EXPOSE Them To It		**Once They EXPERIENCE It**		**That Which EXCITES Them**

Standard: _____

Content: _____

Designation: _____

EVC Minimum:	**Let Them EXPLORE It**	Knowledge & Competence:	**They Will ENGAGE In**	Cultural:
_____ _____ _____	Activities: _____ _____ _____	_____ _____ _____	**Necessary Activity:** Think / Do See / Listen	_____ _____
EVC Maximum:	Strategies: _____ _____	Assignments / Assessments / EVC Statements:	**Likely Questions:** _____ _____ _____	Developmental: _____ _____
_____ _____ _____ _____	Materials: _____ _____ _____	_____ _____ _____ _____	**Likely Difficulty:** _____ _____ _____	Individual: _____ _____
EXPOSE Them To It		**Once They EXPERIENCE It**		**That Which EXCITES Them**

Educational Provision: Possession   /   Understanding   /   Competence   /   Value   /   Success

DESIGN IT
AM I LEADING, PROVOKING, AND SUPPORTING AN EDUCATIONAL PURSUIT?

Standard: _____

Content: _____

Designation: _____

EVC Minimum:	**Let Them EXPLORE It**	Knowledge & Competence:	**They Will ENGAGE In**	Cultural:
_____	Activities:	_____	**Necessary Activity:**	_____
_____	_____	_____	Think / Do	_____
_____	_____	_____	See / Listen	_____
_____	_____	_____	**Likely Questions:**	Developmental:
EVC Maximum:	Strategies:	Assignments / Assessments / EVC Statements:	_____	_____
_____	_____	_____	_____	_____
_____	_____	_____	**Likely Difficulty:**	Individual:
_____	Materials:	_____	_____	_____
_____	_____	_____	_____	_____
EXPOSE Them To It		**Once They EXPERIENCE It**		**That Which EXCITES Them**

Standard: _____

Content: _____

Designation: _____

EVC Minimum:	**Let Them EXPLORE It**	Knowledge & Competence:	**They Will ENGAGE In**	Cultural:
_____	Activities:	_____	**Necessary Activity:**	_____
_____	_____	_____	Think / Do	_____
_____	_____	_____	See / Listen	_____
_____	_____	_____	**Likely Questions:**	Developmental:
EVC Maximum:	Strategies:	Assignments / Assessments / EVC Statements:	_____	_____
_____	_____	_____	_____	_____
_____	_____	_____	**Likely Difficulty:**	Individual:
_____	Materials:	_____	_____	_____
_____	_____	_____	_____	_____
EXPOSE Them To It		**Once They EXPERIENCE It**		**That Which EXCITES Them**

Instructional Level: Caregiver / Teacher / Educator / Profound Mentor / Intense Trainer

DESIGN IT
DID I FACILITATE THE EDUCATIONAL PROCESS AND FULFILL THE MISSION OF EDUCATION?

Unit: _____

Week Of: _____

Standard: _____

Content: _____

Designation: _____

Let Them EXPLORE It

They Will ENGAGE In

EVC Minimum:
_____
_____
_____

EVC Maximum:
_____
_____
_____

EXPOSE Them To It

Activities:
_____
_____

Strategies:
_____
_____

Materials:
_____
_____

Knowledge & Competence:
_____
_____

Assignments / Assessments / EVC Statements:
_____
_____
_____

Once They **EXPERIENCE** It

Necessary Activity:
Think / Do
See / Listen

Likely Questions:
_____
_____

Likely Difficulty:
_____
_____

Cultural:
_____
_____

Developmental:
_____
_____

Individual:
_____
_____

That Which **EXCITES** Them

Standard: _____

Content: _____

Designation: _____

Let Them EXPLORE It

They Will ENGAGE In

EVC Minimum:
_____
_____
_____

EVC Maximum:
_____
_____
_____

EXPOSE Them To It

Activities:
_____
_____

Strategies:
_____
_____

Materials:
_____
_____

Knowledge & Competence:
_____
_____

Assignments / Assessments / EVC Statements:
_____
_____
_____

Once They **EXPERIENCE** It

Necessary Activity:
Think / Do
See / Listen

Likely Questions:
_____
_____

Likely Difficulty:
_____
_____

Cultural:
_____
_____

Developmental:
_____
_____

Individual:
_____
_____

That Which **EXCITES** Them

Educational Provision: Possession   /   Understanding   /   Competence   /   Value   /   Success

DESIGN IT
AM I LEADING, PROVOKING, AND SUPPORTING AN EDUCATIONAL PURSUIT?

Standard: _____

Content: _____

Designation: _____

EVC Minimum:
_____
_____
_____
_____

EVC Maximum:
_____
_____
_____
_____

EXPOSE Them To It

Let Them EXPLORE It

Activities:
_____
_____

Strategies:
_____

Materials:
_____
_____
_____

Knowledge & Competence:
_____
_____
_____

Assignments / Assessments / EVC Statements:
_____
_____
_____
_____

Once They EXPERIENCE It

They Will ENGAGE In

Necessary Activity:
Think / Do
See / Listen

Likely Questions:
_____
_____
_____

Likely Difficulty:
_____
_____
_____

Cultural:
_____
_____
_____

Developmental:
_____
_____

Individual:
_____
_____

That Which EXCITES Them

Standard: _____

Content: _____

Designation: _____

EVC Minimum:
_____
_____
_____
_____

EVC Maximum:
_____
_____
_____
_____

EXPOSE Them To It

Let Them EXPLORE It

Activities:
_____
_____

Strategies:
_____

Materials:
_____
_____
_____

Knowledge & Competence:
_____
_____
_____

Assignments / Assessments / EVC Statements:
_____
_____
_____
_____

Once They EXPERIENCE It

They Will ENGAGE In

Necessary Activity:
Think / Do
See / Listen

Likely Questions:
_____
_____
_____

Likely Difficulty:
_____
_____
_____

Cultural:
_____
_____
_____

Developmental:
_____
_____

Individual:
_____
_____

That Which EXCITES Them

Instructional Level: Caregiver / Teacher / Educator / Profound Mentor / Intense Trainer

DESIGN IT
Did I Facilitate The Educational Process And Fulfill The Mission Of Education?

Unit: _____

Week Of: _____

Standard: _____

Content: _____

Designation: _____

EVC Minimum:	**Let Them EXPLORE It**	Knowledge & Competence:	**They Will ENGAGE In**	Cultural:
_____	Activities:	_____	**Necessary Activity:** Think / Do See / Listen	_____
_____	_____	_____	**Likely Questions:**	_____
EVC Maximum:	Strategies:	**Assignments / Assessments / EVC Statements:**	_____	**Developmental:**
_____	_____	_____	_____	_____
_____	Materials:	_____	**Likely Difficulty:**	Individual:
_____	_____	_____	_____	_____
EXPOSE Them To It		**Once They EXPERIENCE It**		**That Which EXCITES Them**

Standard: _____

Content: _____

Designation: _____

EVC Minimum:	**Let Them EXPLORE It**	Knowledge & Competence:	**They Will ENGAGE In**	Cultural:
_____	Activities:	_____	**Necessary Activity:** Think / Do See / Listen	_____
_____	_____	_____	**Likely Questions:**	_____
EVC Maximum:	Strategies:	**Assignments / Assessments / EVC Statements:**	_____	**Developmental:**
_____	_____	_____	_____	_____
_____	Materials:	_____	**Likely Difficulty:**	Individual:
_____	_____	_____	_____	_____
EXPOSE Them To It		**Once They EXPERIENCE It**		**That Which EXCITES Them**

Educational Provision: Possession / Understanding / Competence / Value / Success

DESIGN IT
AM I LEADING, PROVOKING, AND SUPPORTING AN EDUCATIONAL PURSUIT?

Standard: _____

Content: _____

Designation: _____

EVC Minimum:	**Let Them EXPLORE It** Activities:	Knowledge & Competence:	**They Will ENGAGE In** Necessary Activity: Think / Do See / Listen Likely Questions:	Cultural:
EVC Maximum:	Strategies: Materials:	Assignments / Assessments / EVC Statements:	Likely Difficulty:	Developmental: Individual:
EXPOSE Them To It		**Once They EXPERIENCE It**		**That Which EXCITES Them**

Standard: _____

Content: _____

Designation: _____

EVC Minimum:	**Let Them EXPLORE It** Activities:	Knowledge & Competence:	**They Will ENGAGE In** Necessary Activity: Think / Do See / Listen Likely Questions:	Cultural:
EVC Maximum:	Strategies: Materials:	Assignments / Assessments / EVC Statements:	Likely Difficulty:	Developmental: Individual:
EXPOSE Them To It		**Once They EXPERIENCE It**		**That Which EXCITES Them**

Instructional Level: Caregiver / Teacher / Educator / Profound Mentor / Intense Trainer

DESIGN IT
DID I FACILITATE THE EDUCATIONAL PROCESS AND FULFILL THE MISSION OF EDUCATION?

Unit: _____

Week Of: _____

Standard: _____

Content: _____

Designation: _____

EVC Minimum:
_____
_____
_____
_____

EVC Maximum:
_____
_____
_____
_____

EXPOSE Them To It

Let Them EXPLORE It

Activities:
_____
_____

Strategies:
_____
_____

Materials:
_____
_____

Knowledge & Competence:
_____
_____

Assignments / Assessments / EVC Statements:
_____
_____
_____
_____

Once They EXPERIENCE It

They Will ENGAGE In

Necessary Activity:
Think / Do
See / Listen

Likely Questions:
_____
_____
_____

Likely Difficulty:
_____
_____
_____

Cultural:
_____
_____

Developmental:
_____
_____

Individual:
_____
_____

That Which EXCITES Them

Standard: _____

Content: _____

Designation: _____

EVC Minimum:
_____
_____
_____
_____

EVC Maximum:
_____
_____
_____
_____

EXPOSE Them To It

Let Them EXPLORE It

Activities:
_____
_____

Strategies:
_____
_____

Materials:
_____
_____

Knowledge & Competence:
_____
_____

Assignments / Assessments / EVC Statements:
_____
_____
_____
_____

Once They EXPERIENCE It

They Will ENGAGE In

Necessary Activity:
Think / Do
See / Listen

Likely Questions:
_____
_____
_____

Likely Difficulty:
_____
_____
_____

Cultural:
_____
_____

Developmental:
_____
_____

Individual:
_____
_____

That Which EXCITES Them

Educational Provision: Possession / Understanding / Competence / Value / Success

PROGRESS REPORT

1) When I reflect on what I **EXPOSED** students to this semester, I see that:

I was successful…_____
_____
_____
_____

I really struggled…_____
_____
_____
_____

Moving forward…_____
_____
_____
_____

I may need my allies…_____
_____
_____
_____

2) When I reflect on what and how I let students **EXPLORE** this semester, I see that that:

I was successful…_____
_____
_____
_____

I really struggled…_____
_____
_____
_____

Moving forward…_____
_____
_____
_____

I may need my allies…_____
_____
_____
_____

3) When I reflect on the **EXPERIENCE** I provided students with this semester, I see that:

I was successful…_____
_____
_____
_____

I really struggled…_____
_____
_____
_____

Moving forward…_____
_____
_____
_____

I may need my allies…_____
_____
_____
_____

PROGRESS REPORT

4) When I reflect on how I required/allowed students to **ENGAGE** this semester, I see that:

I was successful…_____
_____
_____

I really struggled…_____
_____
_____

Moving forward…_____
_____
_____

I may need my allies…_____
_____
_____
_____

5) When I reflect on what I did to **EXCITE** students this semester, I see that:

I was successful…_____
_____
_____

I really struggled…_____
_____
_____

Moving forward…_____
_____
_____

I may need my allies…_____
_____
_____

6) When I reflect on my **EDUCATIONAL PROVISION** and **INSTRUCTIONAL LEVEL**, I see that:

I was successful…_____
_____
_____

I really struggled…_____
_____
_____

Moving forward…_____
_____
_____

I may need my allies…_____
_____
_____
_____

GLOSSARY OF TERMS

Accountable – being anchored by and firmly attached to an obligation or responsibility.

Active Participant – student persona resembling a permissive readiness to observe the instruction of educational leadership energetically and optimistically in hopes of acquiring a high-quality education.

Adolescence – a transitional phase, between childhood and adulthood, where one's ability to prove they can control and be responsible for their life, by doing things appropriately and efficiently with a high probability of success, allows those with partial control and responsibility for their life and livelihood to give up control and responsibility fully.

Adolescent – one who has attained limited control and responsibility for their life and livelihood because of increased learning, understanding, maturing, education in the study of life, and the limited ability to do things appropriately and efficiently with a good probability of success.

Adult – one who has attained full control and responsibility for their life and livelihood because of superior learning, understanding, maturing, education in the study of life, and the ability to do things appropriately and efficiently with a high probability of success.

Adulthood – a phase of life after adolescence where superior learning, understanding, maturing, education in the study of life, and the ability to do things appropriately and efficiently with a high probability of success allow one to have full control and responsibility for their life and livelihood.

Advocate – the recognition of a position of weakness and vulnerability paired with an offering of supportive actions meant to defend and protect.

Ally – an individual, entity, or institution that has a joint interest and agrees to partner with another in their pursuit of a goal.

Authority – having the permission or being in the position to deny or grant the allowance of using power.

Caregiver – one who is focused on fulfilling the basic needs of a child.

GLOSSARY OF TERMS

Certified – considered to be educated by an officially authorized governing body or agency in a particular area or field of study.

Child – one whose life and livelihood are the responsibility of another more than they are for themself, because of their need for learning, understanding, maturing, and an education in the study of life.

Childhood – a transitional phase in a child's life, before adolescence, where the exploration of curiosity leads to learning, understanding, maturing, and an education in the study of life that prompts those responsible for their life and livelihood to give them limited control and responsibility over their own life.

Classroom Management – a teacher's ability to assess how well the academic environment provides space and opportunity for the exposure to, exploration of, and experience with an education, and steer experiences away from low levels of effectiveness while pushing toward higher levels.

Demand – to make an official request from a position of authority and refuse to be denied.

Discipline – the process of putting someone under control.

Education – a unique assortment of information that one possesses, understands, knows how to use, and benefits from (qualitatively).

Educate – to take the lead in a focused effort to assist students in their pursuit of an education.

Educated – possessing qualitative evidence of an acquired education.

Educator – one who, intentionally, teaches lessons and plans activities that allow students to be exposed to, explore, and experience an education to provoke and support them in pursuing and acquiring an education.

Educational Value Continuum™ – a scale that documents and expresses how one could use and benefit from a variety of functions and possibilities contained within academic information once that content has been possessed and understood.

GLOSSARY OF TERMS

Engaged Agent – student persona embodying an acute preparation to adhere to the educational process eagerly and expectantly with aspirations of acquiring full mastery of the educational possibility.

Fun – enjoyment of an experience.

Graduate – one who is ready, prepared, and qualified for an advanced educational level by becoming certified as a successful student on the previous learning level.

Grievance – a specific complaint filed with righteous authority for the purpose of solving a problem.

Hypocrisy – professing a standard or belief that one's character or behavior fails to support.

Influence – the persuasive energy of one's power, authority, and/or resources that act on or prompt another.

Integrity – having thoughts, words, and actions that all resemble the same thing.

Intense Trainer – educator persona exemplifying astute intuition while demonstrating supreme proficiency and mastery of a high-quality education.

Miseducation of Education™ – an endemic issue plaguing the education system caused by a failure to explicitly define "education," which produces and perpetuates obstructions to the productivity, possibility, and promise of the system: disallowing any assurance that progression through an institution's academic program is purposed for acquiring an education.

Noble – held and regarded in a class or rank esteemed highly above others because of one's distinguished excellence.

Parent – one who takes responsibility for a child's life, livelihood, growth, and development while providing safe, appropriate space and opportunity for that child to explore their curiosity while becoming more knowledgeable and experienced in areas where learning, understanding, and maturing are necessary.

Power – the ability to do.

GLOSSARY OF TERMS

Prepared – fulfillment of the internal and external prerequisites necessary to accomplish a thing.

Profound Mentor – educator persona exhibiting keen insight while demonstrating practical integration of a high-quality education.

Pupil – one who is willing to submit to instruction and participate in learning.

Qualified – possessing educational abilities and evidence that project and predict probable success.

Ready – acknowledgment of an internal desire and willingness to accomplish a thing.

Righteous Authority – being properly positioned with and connected to a higher source of authority and, thereby, permitted to allow or deny the usage of power to those dependent upon you.

School – a designated area that provides space and opportunity to be exposed to, explore, and experience an education.

Student – one who actively engages in the pursuit of an education.

Success – the achievement/accomplishment of one's goal(s).

Supply & Demand Education™ – an educational philosophy stipulating that the explicit defining of "education" allows the learner/instructor relationship, and the institutional exchange of learning/instructing, to be stabilized by the fundamental principles of economics; thus, enhancing the system's immunity to the *Miseducation of Education*™.

Teaching – the utilization of knowledgeable lessons and/or activities to instruct an intellectual minor in an academic discipline, practical ability, or vocational skill set.

Teacher – one who provides an intellectual minor with an understanding of knowledge previously unfamiliar through teaching.

ABOUT THE AUTHOR

Daniel C. Manley is an American educator, author, speaker, and educational provocateur who has made it his life's work to make the attainment of a high-quality education a real possibility for all young people. As a mentor, teacher, and administrator, he has served the middle school and high school population for nearly twenty years. As Co-Founder and CEO of Stand & Withstand Integrity Group, he has made it his mission to empower and prepare children to be firmly planted, deeply rooted, and properly positioned as adults with an education that allows for them to achieve practical success.

<u>Coming Soon</u>
INSPECT IT:
What "Guess What I Learned At School Today" Really Means

USE IT & BENEFIT:
Functions & Possibilities of an Education Series

Become *Supply & Demand Education*™ Certified
Stand & Withstand Integrity Group LLC
P.O. Box 782771
Wichita, KS 67278

CONTACT@STANDWITHSTAND.ORG

DEDICATION:

To every teacher who has ever worked to plan a lesson enriched with educational value. Allow this guide to help you to design such an experience.